HUMAN DIGNITY
AND
NATIONAL IDENTITY

ESSENTIAL FOR SOCIAL ETHICS

JEMISIK CULTURAL BOOKS LTD.

HUMAN DIGNITY
AND
NATIONAL IDENTITY

ESSENTIAL FOR SOCIAL ETHICS

Rev. Dr. Timothy Murere Njoya, The. Dip., M. Div., Ph.D.

First published in 1987 by
Jemisik Cultural Books
Balfour House,
Kimathi Street
P.O. Box 67346
NAIROBI.

Printed by
Press Trust Printers Ltd.
Dar-es-Salaam Road, Industrial Area,
P.O. Box 18485
NAIROBI.

ISBN 9966-858-05-9

CONTENTS

INTRODUCTION

If you look at the whole situation in Africa, *where Kenya is situated,* you may find that people are trying to study, rule, develop, bear children and get rich without any purpose of doing so because they do not have a national ethical standard from which to derive their own. This ethical standard that is missing is HUMAN DIGNITY. All other forms of ethics, not derived from this one of human dignity are interim, and may be null and void.

On the surface, Africa appears to live according to interim ethics of submission to forces of alien self-interests which people follow blindly while at the same time hoping to see them die. We are very happy that colonialism has died. Millions of Christians who want no ethical responsibilities for famines, wars, poverty, disase, corruption and tribalism think of life in terms of the "world to come" and some welcome catastrophes and disasters as signs of the second coming of Christ. This irresponsible and escapist attitude gives impression that Africans live in a world which is not theirs. My book of human dignity wants to end this confusion by telling our people to free themselves from unethical forces whose origin they do not know.

Underneath the surface of this ethical cover-up Africans have a permanent ethic which does not excuse them to follow others irresponsibly. The nature of our human dignity is that it has endured many historical transitions, or interims, and has survived pre-colonial, colonial and post-colonial traumas triumphantly. It is quite realistic to follow the African dignity which has conquered humiliation, slavery, exploitation, oppression and abuse of human rights and succeeded to emerge alive and well. Only an ethic based on this human dignity can help us have good religious, educational, political, economic and national values.

When western powers termed Jomo Kenyatta and other freedom fighters rebels, terrorists and immoral, our ethics of human dignity termed them liberators and heroes. When Jesus Christ, acting in a similar situation was declared a rebellious crimimal and nailed on the cross, he died and rose again which proved the interim ethics of that time null and void. This is not to claim that all drop-outs, rebels, dissidents and critics of any system have a visionary goal in life, but that there should be an ethic that stands the test of time and respects man as having been created in the image of God. Those who want to avoid ethics in their work, family and institutions should know that their "ethics of avoidance" is what is landing us in our sex, business, educational, political, management and other problems.

In this book I have attempted to present human dignity as what makes people want to continue living and unites them to work together as a people of one nation to make their common life worth living. A nation without one common ethic that constitutes its national identity is like a person without soul, conscience and self-respect.

I look forward to a time when the power of dignity that holds tribes, clans and cultural groups together, shall fully concentrate on holding the nation together. Our people used to think of human dignity as the spiritual force that made human life unique and produced the institutions that provided that life with security. The African dignity expressed itself in personality as loyalty to the tribe. Life without dignity lacked the moral and spiritual virtues necessary for being a member of the tribe. A person without dignity was not only a dander to himself but also to the tribe (nation). This means that the African derived his ethic from respect, obedience, kindness and allegiance to his nation. And why should the African of today have an ethic derived in profit making and personal gains?

In the village community where I grew up, old people of my grandparents'age, used to say that life in the village was more dignified with the bodies of the dead which the villagers had to throw into the bushes for hyenas to eat than with the living bodies of wicked and evil people who hated, robbed, abused, raped, killed, exploited, oppressed, cheated and betrayed others, disturbing the peace of everybody in the community for selfish reasons. Even in the Bible, virtues of dignity consist of having communion and fellowship with others. The Bible considers sinners as the outsiders who interfere with God's kingdom and who God will ostricize from his. kingdom to hell for "hyenas" to consume.

Human dignity is the only conditions through which anyone is allowed to enjoy the rights and freedom of his country. In Israel where faith in God and·obedience to his laws were considered essential measurements of national identity, all Kings, Priests and Prophets, together with their followers, who worshipped idols lost their rights to live in Israel and were taken into Babylonian captivity. The integrity of the nation depended mainly on the dignity of its people, not on wealth, military and wisdom.

The book presents two ways of exercising dignity, personal and collective, that is, individual and corporate. When a mother gives her child food, she exercises her dignity in love. But when the judge passes a right sentence to an accused person he exercises his dignity as justice. Love is what a person does for the benefit of another voluntarily and at his own cost, while justice is the same love when done by a person on duty in his professional capacity. When we demonstrate love privately this is not enough until we demonstrate it as justice when acting as chiefs, teachers, priests, doctors, presidents, merchants and police while on public duty. This is why the idea of national identity is, in this book, a paramount issue. When it comes to showing love to our children we have no problems building hospitals and schools for them, but that love is useless and counterproductive if it does not build schools and hospitals where children of other people can benefit. Once you make love national, it becomes justice. It is impossible for a country to prosper and progress unless we build common institutions to benefit the present and future generations.

This means that the nation is myself and my family enlarged and extended to embrace even those my tribe never included. The nation represents my identity and in bigger form, having stronger hands, feet and ears than mine, and therefore extending my dignity more effectively. Think of the Voice of Kenya as your voice, the civil service as your hands and the state as your head. The nation has a religious institution that acts as a national conscience beyond the abilities of an individual believer. Just as a man of dignity is useless confronting a gang of thieves full of vanity, dignity is useless unless it is a national ethic. The nation, and no longer the clan or tribe, is the body that expresses our common dignity and makes us all feel equal. If one offends the nation he violates his own dignity and if he offends his neighbour the nation must intervene because its own integrity is affected. This is why the community, which had no prisons during the pre-colonial era, used to ostricize certain disrespectful criminals to unknown places beyond the boundaries of the tribe to make sure that whatever might befall them their blood did not contaminate the tribal soil or tarnish the sacred image of the tribe.

Chapter four deals with how to communicate dignity to our children and the impact culture has in this endeavour. The psychology and philosophy of children development based on human dignity is essential for all homes, schools, churches and public institutions. Infact, chapter five deals with things that bring moral dilemma to our youth and illustrates this with the sex morality of a girl a doctor made pregnant.

There many questions raised in the book about human life in general and specifically about issues of "mercy-killing', sex and marriage, and participation in national political systems. One may ask, can human dignity be human if it is not enriched by the natural dignity of the forests, animals and spaces that sorround us and the whole creation? Readers may find more questions than these in the book and seek answers where mine are not satisfactory.

Finally, let me take this opportunity to say that the ideas presented in this book are not the monopoly of one person, culture and nation and may be there and expressed differently in other African countries and the rest of the world. Thanks to my Spiritual Revival and church background I could not avoid religious inclinations when writing, and due to academic experience here in Kenya and elsewhere in America these inclinations have a Western Cultural bias. I feel grateful to my wife and children with whom I have shared these ideas in their formative stage and to the Family Life Education Programme of the National Christian Council of Kenya in whose seminars some of these ideas were first publicly discussed, and to Mrs. Josephine Mathenge and her family whose generous offer to type the manuscripts speeded up my work to author the book. Every thought expressed in this book is my own mind.

August 1987   *T. M. Njoya*

CHAPTER I
WHAT IS DIGNITY?

1.1 HOW AND IN WHAT WAYS DOES DIGNITY EXIST?

Human dignity is the pleasure, joy, love and respect of life for its own sake. Dignity is the end to which everything, even survival itself is a means. Human diginity is a life worh to live. It is what unites people to work together to improve the conditions of their existence. The nation is the result of the work and relationships by which people lift themselves to the highest state of human fulfilment and satisfaction. This is what makes human digity and national identity as two sides of the same coin.

While human dignity is unique, it is apart of the universal dignity of all creatures, both living and no-living. The fact that human dignity is derived from natural and social conditions of existence makes it able to extend into the national environment into which one is born and raised, beyond individual personality, to form national identity. We shall therefore discuss human dignity as the highest quality of life which people can attain and sustain by use of their resources of mind. time and material to form national identity.

Human dignity expresses itself in personality as self-confidence, self-respect and self-esteem and in national identity in the form of morality, order, freedom, love, peace, unity and justice. What is love in personal relationship becomes justice in social relationships. In this sense we cannot think of dignity as existing in a person who pursues self-interests at the expense of other's interests. Neither can we think of it as a national dignity any form of national development which does not achieve dignity for all.

Human dignity is always more than a personal and private possession because it extends beyond the physical body into the life of a community, family, church or nation. Only when in the form of national identity can dignity endure extreme conditions of mental, spiritual and physical torture without giving up its own self-respect and self-confidence. Dignity tells the one it dignifies that even if you die for what is right, true and beautiful, others in your nation shall benefit. For instance, there were Kenyans who during the struggle for independence regarded suffering and dying for their country as the noblest and highest form of dignity. They would not have accepted to die for themselves as nobody can offer to die for oneself at all. Those our national ancestors let go their own properties and sacrificed their lives to free their country from indignity. Indignity was for them the devaluation of life below levels human beings could accept to live. Our parents therefore endured persecution, detention, deprivation and affliction without bitterness because they were fighting for their own dignity in terms of national identity. Dignity is the final end to which all living, work and things are sacrificed. It is the unity of body, mind and soul. To that which gives your life meaning and purpose, to that you offer yourself and everything in your possession, because that constitutes your dignity.

If people believed that when a priest commits their bodies to the grave, soil to soil, ashes to ashes, and dust to dust, that is all they are worth and nothing else, nobody would worry about national development. Dignity makes us apart of the social and historical conditions that outline our own bodily existence. This does not mean that dignity has a spiritual existence disembodied from our physical existence, but that when we cease to live it continues to live in the memories, culture and history of the nation and society to which we belonged. The dignity of our ancestors continues in our lives and reflects itself in the language, art, infrastructures and systems we inherited from them.

However, human dignity is not limited to social and historical life. Human dignity extends to the general dignity of the whole universe of known and unknown things, magical and real, visible and invisible, immenent and trascendent, natural and supernatural, physical and spiritual, earthly and heavenly things. Africans used to recognize stars, planets, winds, rivers, animals, events, concepts, energies, spirits, and God as having elements of human dignity within their own essence. But other than God, none of these other things had dignity equal or higher than that of man. Man's dignity derives a lot of meaning and fulfilment in this association with things in the universe. This means that dignity shifts with culture, environment and time. In Kenya, Maasai moranism which expresses the dignity of a culture will slowly become replaced with other expressions of national dignity like education, Central governments, common laws and monetory economy. Any change in the things one sees, hears, touches and smells, shift from traditional to scientific and technological modernization, even the improvement of access to water, food and wealth will alter the human perception of dignity.

Human dignity is at variance with imported ideas which equate man with the external things he possesses. *Human dignity exists in being, not in having.* People and not the things they have consitute their dignity and national identity. The prophets and apostles of Christ, who had nothing to offer for others to have dignity, offered themselves. Dignity takes the form of self-sacrificial love to improve the moral, spiritual, economic and political conditions of existenece for others. What we do for the future generations becomes the token of our sacrifice to them in thanksgiving for what the past generations of dedicated servants did for us. In doing this we must not over-emphasize the dignity of one generation to the extent of depriving the future generations life in a natural environment free of pollution and exploitation. Human dignity is not completely detached from the dignity of crocodiles, hyenas, butterflies and other creatures in the ecosystem. Any abuse or misuse of these for selfish ends may drive our children an essential part of human dignity. *Development and nature are partners, not enemies.* The protection of trees, ant, snakes, fish, water, air and soil is an essential part of self-respect. Modernization should be a process of dignity our environment and recognition that "everything that God made was good." Unless we Kenyans preserve our natural forests, wild animals and other things as evidence of our dignity we shall lose the intergrity of our national identity. We can gain more respect by respecting our old mother nature than satisfying our greed for materia wealth. It is like to rape ones' mother to disrespect our beautiful natural environment. Before we are social, cultual and historical we are environmental. This is why we have normadic culture in the arid and semi-arid areas and settled agricultural culture in the arable areas. Environment shapes our politics, religion, social institutions and the general way of life. It is to adopt ourselves to the natural environment that we have scientific and technological innovations, such as irrigation, industry, communication and urbanization. Will the over-population destroy the environment and therefore destroy human dignity?

The difference between independence and colonialism is measured not by how wealthier and bigger we are now than we used to be, but by whether we are more fulfiled now than then. We have nobody to hate because nobody hates us. The only struggle against others that we now have is against our own selfish tendencies toward becoming fascists, dictators and robbers. If these tendencies are not defeated by the positive ones of love, peace and justice we shall become our own self-colonizers. Next to the preservation of natural environment as our source of dignity we must therefore maintain the politics, laws and religion that guarantee man his freedom of expression and means of existence. The work which a sweeper, vendor shoeshiner, soldiers, doctors, priest or teacher does provide him his livelihood and gives him his dignity. Between a taxi driver and an airbus captain are common legal and ethical standards that make them both equal members of our national identity. A street sweeper carrying a broom is as respectable as a soldier carrying his gun. A newspaper vendor thrives on communicating the directives of our president as much as our president thrives on his directive reaching the masses through the vendor. I know of an employer who nearly killed himself because of hearing that an employee he had dismissed from his employment due to gross misconduct had died in a motor accident before finding another job. This means that there are national principles and laws of national identity that provide for common dignity despite day-to-day human differences.

This means that we examine our social institutions, economic organizations and religious structures and see whether they provide ethical directions conducive to human dignity and national identity. Once we are able to recognize human dignity as more than the personal property of chosen individuals, and as a unique value universal to all people, then we can modify our social, national and religious systems to reinforce dignity. Nations should exist solely for the function of safeguarding and sustaining only those institutions that create, develop and enhance human dignity. *National identity is the total dignity of all the people who constitute the nation* and falls or rises with the fall or rise of human dignity. A nation preserves itself only by preserving the dignity of its people and when it sees no other value to exchange any life of a human being.

Once each and every person believes that his life and dignity are embodied in the national identity of his country he will love the name of his country like his own personal name. This vicarious nature of the nation as a personality that embodies all its citizens into a common nationality will eliminate tribalism, clanish feelings, parochialism and divisiveness. Vices that root from multiple identities and conflicting ideologies will cease when all Kenyans will have a common image. *When we speak of the image of God we are describing a common source of identity from which the people of all races and nationalities derive their dignity.* This universal image manifests itself locally in national identity.

The reason millions of Africans prefer to become refugees in foreign countries is because they believe their governments to have lost their national identity and given way to tribal, clan or other exclusive identities. Rather than remain victims of narrow identities some refugees organize to return home with a national identity by overthrowing those who had caused them to flee. A nation lasts as long as and no longer than it is able to maintain itself as one family consisting of those born and welcome in it. As the highest and largest family of self-preservation and self-interests, the nation recognizes no other forms of self-interests and self-preservation in it than its own.

If it does recognize many interests besides the common interest of all its citizens those injured by others interests lack protection. Even the laws of nature and God, which are higher than national laws, allow a creature to flee from danger and defend itself according to the laws of the jungle. This means that actions like *abortion to kill an unborn baby who cannot flee from the mother,* wars in which people are rendered helpless and ghettos where people die of hunger and malnutrition amidst plenty of food reflect national indignity and vanity, not dignity.

The image of God in man provides him with a national identity which frees him from obedience to oaths, laws, contracts, duties and obligations that compel him to hurt himself or his neighbour to achieve any end other than to protect oneself from getting killed. Any custom, tradition, force or authority that requires a man to infringe upon another's life or dignity has exceeded its legitimate power. One is not bound by treaties or vows that elevate him above or lower him below another person. This is what gives justification to fight against Apartheid in South Africa. Any person denied his dignity may opt to die in the struggle to regain his dignity. *Life without dignity is not worth living.* To me, the cross means refusing any terms of existence that would extend human life on earth beyond the point at which people accept to forfeit their essence as human beings, thus to surrender their dignity. The Bible considers people without dignity as the living dead for whom the sacrifice of Christ was necessary to restore their dignity.

1.2 IN WHAT WAYS DO WE MANIFEST DIGNITY

We have succeeded to display a national model of dignity based on such essential characteristics of human self-consciousness, self-esteem, self-confidence and self-respect. Until 1964 I used to think of human dignity as something like the chief's status, crown and title which the chief would lose if dismissed from his position. Sometimes dignity appeared to me as something like a physically strong and handsome man or a beautiful middle aged woman. But in 1964, as a first year in the Theological College I was elected the chairman of the Catering Committee. My duties were to supervise cooks and cleaners in the Kitchen and dining hall. One day woman cleaner came to me running and screaming as if chased by a lion. Before asking her what was the problem she said "look at those students walking into the dining hall with muddy boots. They are insulting my dignity. They have no manners. Supposing I spilt ink in their written examination paper?"

I saw that this woman identified herself with her work so much that she considered the muddy boots on her clean floor as worse than a disease in her body. I observed foam coming out of her mouth and about to fall down out of hysteria. She said, "These students are ruining my life. They are no better than the white colonialists who used to mistreat us. If this is the kind of African leaders to replace the white colonial rulers I shall hang myself." At that point I saw the matter was more serious than I had imagined. I realized that she had no other role to play in the independent Kenya other than sweep and clean the floor. For her, independence meant not the change of job but respect, esteem, rcognition, an appreciation for what she had to offer. But this meaning of independence, as love, respect and esteem lacked the kind of the dignity the love, respect and esteem for one another was not available from the theological students. They lacked the kind of dignity the cleaner expected from them. She stopped crying when I told her that those students were the products of colonial education who wish to play the role of the colonial master. She was even more surprised to hear from me that her screaming awakened in me a sense of dignity. Today, I am like her, my work is the means by which I affirm my dignity. It is a call of dignity to serve my people. It was her call of dignity to serve as a sweeper. It was Jesus' call of dignity to wash his disciples feet. It was that woman's self-consciousness, self-respect and self-confidence that constituted her dignity. It was that dignity that the satanic behaviour of the theological students trod down upon. They had failed to recognize that her work was an expression and extension of her dignity. The consciousness of and for dignity is not something Africans would have inherited from their colonial rulers but something which gave rise to their struggle. The spirit of those who organised themselves into parties, churches, associations and groups for expressing their common dignity transformed itself into national identity. It brought together the various tribal, clan class and regional interests to form common national interests. Squatters, labourers and peasants lost their ethnic identities and gained a new consciousness of being Kenyan. This common birth, due to the struggle against a common external enemy is no longer the only one that binds the people together. Today, people are bound together by the fact that they have identified themselves with the nation and national aspirations. Independence created a new dynamic in which the idea of having a common enemy was replaced with the one of having a common national identity. The national identity is in a formal sense codified in the constitutional and the sessional Paper No 10 of 1965, This national identity may take many forms like serving in the Armed Forces, farming, teaching, social work, preaching, catering, mechanics, carpentry, painting, curving, or nursing but in the final analysis it is what one does with his life, how he spends it that counts for national dignity. This national dignity is antithetical and antagonistic to all racial, clannish, class or sectional identities that tend to erode the power of national identity.

For this reason national dignity must be guarded and protected against fascism, dictatorship and militarism. These may not be our immediate problems but to ignore such tendencies would constitute the greatest threat to our dignity. Human dignity must be pursued as the spiritual foundation of nationhood by which we and our future generations shall bless themselves. Our institutions, social structure, political and economic systems are merely the external manifestations of who we are as a people and a nation. If we lose dignity these institutional manifestations can become instruments of evil where our group uses them to subdue, oppress exploit or destroy the others' dignity.

What, then, is the relationship between human dignity and national identity? When our personal dignity feels secure in the hands of the national constitution and government the immediate thing that comes in our minds is that the nation is ours and we identify ourselves with it. But our understanding of national identity is deeper than this. We identify with our country no matter who is in power. If a fascist takes control over the state, our national dignity takes the form of getting rid of the fascist power. A Ugandan preacher once told me that Ugandans are like Italians, sick and tired of rallying around one leader after another, season after season and year after year and must now rally around their national flag as the best expression of national identity.

The reason I had to return to my country after eight years of my studies in Princeton Seminary, in America was because Americn values did not contribute to my national identity. My judgement of what was good or bad in America was based on what my clan and tribe in Kenya would have valued as good or bad according to their African criteria. I continued to identify myself with whatever happened in Kenya because my mind could measure its value of right or wrong. I blamed myself for the evils of my country and felt proud of its good because my mind consisted of both the good and bad that came from my country. I felf my self as much responsible for the failures of my country as its successes. There was no rise or fall of my country which was not my own. I lived in America like Moses in the court of Pharoah and like Israel in Babylon. The name of Kenya and my name sounded different but represented the one same identity. I discoverd that it was my name and those of others from and in Kenya that collectively made the name of Kenya. This applied to America as well. If Americans were unkind, I thought of their country as unkind. This was due to my tribal influence in which the tribe considered personal behaviour as a good or bad image of his family or tribal character. The new National identity is like a young tree having roots, in the soil enriched by many decayed tribal traditions. The old must die to provide seed and humus for the new.

In the last one hundred years or so, Kenya has experienced the birth, growth and phenomenal development of men and women with identities like my own, with their clans and tribes furnishing them with the background material by which to form national identity. I myself do not regard it as obsence or

9

delegatory to say that my national identity is a resurrection of the dead tribal identitty. From our old traditional identities we have gained inspiration to make national identity the basis of our new dignity, more beautiful, pure and perfect than we have ever read about in the Bible, in the Koran or in the History of Western civilization, and which if we are not careful can be destroyed by sin like that of Adam and Eve. While every dignity has an objective criteria, for example, Christ, empire ideology or church, none of these fully covers all Kenyans. Our christian identity tells us that heaven is our home. Our national identity tells us that Kenya is our home.

I am happy to belong to the present generation of Africans which has created more independent nations than any other race in world history and has founded more new institutions than all other nations of the world. The founding work may take another two or more generation to complete, but it may not have to cost them more severe sacrifices as it has cost us to develop our countries from clan and tribal identities to national identity. May be time will come when ideological identity that is, socialist or capitalist identities, shall be more significant than national identity, but at present, it has cost us blood, sweat, disappointment and frustrations to achieve a better identity than our previous clan identities. Meanwhile, we do live in Africa, in particular Kenya, feel satisfied to project our hard won dignity in relation to our national sovereignity.

1.3 CAN THERE BE DIGNITY BY EXTENSION:

Human beings try to extend their dignity to the institutions and systems by which they reproduce and preserve themselves. When they are born they take time to become conscious of their own identity as individuals. At first their identity is wrapped up with their surroundings, parents and everybody. Once their personality grows and they become conscious of their uniqueness as individuals they then extend this uniqueness to the people they love, their families and their nation. Indeed the nation is the greatest extent to which individuals can entrust their security, health and existence to another institution than their own family. To that which you can surrender your life and feel secure to that you extend your dignity and feel yourself fully represented.

"No one can serve two masters, for either he will hate the one and love the other." Consequently there must be harmony and unity between oneself and the institution or thing to which one feels loyal and represented. Equally true, human dignity cannot continue to be loyal to the old tribal and clan systems which used to unite and protect one's grandparents while these have ceased to be his means of self-preservation and security. The nation has replaced traditional institutions as a viable and effective system of human existence and become the sole institution by which the whole population of a particular and given country can identify itself.

This means that we have eliminated the tribe, clan, class, sectional groupings, castes and parochialism as means of existence. These are no longer capable of projecting the dignity of any people. They threaten and feel threatened by others. National development in Kenya is aimed at achieving a common national identity by which all citizens can measure their true and authentic self without being exclusive of others. However, young nations like Kenya cannot afford to waste the wealth of cultural experience gained through centuries of struggle and tradition. They should therefore look for moral values from their clans and tribes in order to formulate new and modern values. The old decayed values should provide rich humus materials to fertilize and make grow the modern values. In fact the decay of the old tribal and clan religious, political and economic values should be seen not as something obscene but as something which grew mature, died of age and left seeds which can germinate. What values appeared to be tribal or clannish at home should be used as national values. No one should feel phony and guilty because he has a tribal language or character when representing his nation to another nation. The nation is the clan and tribe by extension and elimination. But the nation is not its people by elimination, only by extension. It also represents the family and therefore is family by extension and compliment.

Since dignity cannot be exported or imported, but must be gained through common struggle, sharing of means and methods of existence and collective activities to improve ones community, one cannot have dignity in a nation that denies him opportunity to contribute to its development or in a nation to which he does not wish to offer his service.

Dignity is extended to someone else, to a family or nation into which you want to put some of yourself, to which you give your own life, so that, you can love it like you love yourself. Anyone unable to realize his dignity within his community or nation cannot be expected to represent its image correctly in relation to the rest of the world. Traitors, double-dealers and sell-outs are men or women worse than enemies because they pretend to belong to a nation or community which they hate. They lack in the nation a legitimate framework of reference to their identity and therefore prefer to destroy their own nation in search of another imanginary identity. So, failure to extend ones dignity beyond oneself to an institution more capable, viable and qualified to protect our lives than ourselves is a form of self-worship that believes in itself as the only existence.

Dignity is in this sense behaviour appropriate for each person in order to enhance others' survival. The community is the sole judge of what is appropriate behaviour. Even the *freedom of religion or press must operate within those limits set by the cmmunity or nation as the ones enhancing the dignity of all* its members. Some industrial behaviour may be the extension of some people's wish to become rich at the expense of spoiling the environment and polluting the air and water for others. Such a behaviour lacks dignity in that the industrialists act like a clan tribe or caste within the nation and lack nation identity in their wishes.

Any modernization or industrialization aimed at aping, imitating and copying progress from others who consider themselves more progressive and civilized than yourselves substracts freedom and self-determination from our dignity and achieves under-development. It makes us extensions of other people and leaves us as shadows, stooges and puppets of foreign gods. Dignity cannot be achieved by trying to over-extend ourselves beyond our capacity, potential and ability to accomplish our goals. There is no dignity in the attempt to become like someone else. Once we borrow the behaviour or progress of others we become their slaves. We start to depend on their loans, grants in aid, charity, volunteers, peace corps and missionaries to help us maintain behaviour and identities alien to ours. Catching up with others in their armed race, religions and affluence helps them to use us as sources of raw material and cheap markets for the industrial, technological and ideological materials, military and office software.

In the book, "Ghana The End of an Illusion," the writers tried to expose the technological, political and economic illusion that led to the overthrow of Kwame Nkrumah. Ghana had started its development from as a highly industrial position, in her mind, as London and Paris, and worked herself down to ruins, in reality, the megalomaniac desires and tastes of Ghana's planners to look as big as their former colonizers almost ruined Ghana's identity of a sovereign nation. To the extent to which one extends himself without the centre falling apart, to that extent is dignity maintained and developed. The ability to manage a nation to become what it can support with its resources derives from inner self-confidence and self-respect. One's sovereignty and one's dignity are continuous and coterminous with each other.

In order to retain dignity, individuals must accept their capacities and abilities as the only means by which to extend themselves economically, socially and intellectually. In this respect, nations are no different from people. To remain sovereign and orderly nations must apply self-discipline and control over their expectations, aspirations and goals, otherwise they might violate their dignity trying to become like other nations. If a ten year old child attempts to behave like a forty year old person he burns more energies and destroys the potential of what he would be. He ends up suffering mental depressions because of exhaustion and frustrations.

Many of our Five-Year-Development-Plans, were based on illusions and not on our abilities and capacities to tax ourselves. Some families, living in slum areas of immigrant urbanites planned to have three cars per family under circumstances that discouraged development by encouraging consumption. Slaves cannot be free until they are free from both their physical and external masters and their spiritual and psychological masters. The latter, are the most difficult to get rid of because they consist of hists, desires and urges to become like their masters. For colonized people to be free from their coloniars they must be also be free from their experience of fighting so that they can relax and re-assess their goals. Unless I am free from both the master and the war colonies by which I overthrow him, I cannot settle to enjoy my peace. I must be free from both fighting and the thing I fought against in order to know who I am and be able to enjoy my victory. Failure to get rid of war strategies and the system I fought against will only make me a substitute and replacement of that system. Like father, like son, in some independent countries, those who fought against their colonial masters ended up being like them, having already inherited the very positions, relations, values, religions, and mentalities of masters.

However, there were others whose dignity was formed by the struggle itself because their aim was to produce a nation in their own likeness and image, not to inherit one. Consequently, we have a few nastionalists whose names are too controversial to mention who saw the birth of a nation in their struggle, and not as a gift from overseas. Their example was only capable of renouncing their traditional tribal, clan, racial, and caste identities in order to fashion one based on national behaviour. They formed a national party more able than the clan, family and tribe to hold complex behaviour like heterogeneity in homegeneity, plurality in unity, multiplicity in singularity and religions diversity in secular neutrality. This helped people to abandon their traditional customs and taboos in favour of constitutional laws and common interests. The nation, in the process of this tansformation, becomes a melting pot in which ethnic, class and parochial identities become sifted, ground, kneaded and baked to become edible for everyone. There are Kenyans due to their lack of historical and cultural identity in Kenya also lack strong Kenya economic identity as a result of which they bank their profits outside. While there are areas of national integration like

14

fighting famine and harambee where people of India, Pakistan, Arabia and European back-grounds join Africans in common national interests, in cultural events they isolate and seclude themselves into social castes. This makes their national identity incomplete. During national days, millions of Kenyans from all ethnic and racial backgrounds celebrate their independence and unity as a sovereign people, unique and one in space, and proud of their common history, inalienable rights to own in common their geographical boundaries. I once thought of myself as having a higher dignity than a Malawian or Cameroonian who has less territorial space to claim than a Kenyan and wished I were a Zairean, Ethiopian or Nigerian in order to increase my identity.

But dignity does not increase in terms of space, wealth and military might but in terms of fulfilment and satisfaction with what one has. May be the influence of Dr. Kwme Nkrumah about wishing Africa to become a "Super Power" with big bombs was too much in my head. I later discovered that even smaller nations can extend their vanity beyond their boundaries like nazism, zionism and apartheid. A small nation can have as much dignity as a big one, and a big one be as evil as a small one.

Hence, the aim of extending our personal and individual dignity beyond tribal and clan identity is not to form a bigger tribe or clan but to include into national dignity those that tribalism and clannism might exclude. It is due to their factionalism, sectionalism and divisiveness that club-like, clan and tribal identities are evil, but not due to their size, poverty or weakness, it is due to tribal identity that one set of leaders come into power and destroy the history, movements, establishments and institutions of the previous one and set up it own nonsense. National identity follows the Nyayo (footsteps) of the history of the previous leaders, whether bad or good, learns from the bad in order to avoid mistakes and improves on good. Even the millions of refugees who are found everywhere in Africa do feel a sense of national identity connected with the nations they are forced to vacate by their civil conflicts. You can hear them say "We are running away

15

from those dictators, not from our mother land."

Nevertheless not every one who resides and works in Africa, or is black, automatically acquires an African national identity as an expression of his dignity. Identity is more than a sentimental and sensational feeling. It is a social consciousness that may have little to do with genetic origins. We may share genetic and sentimental connections with Africans who are less African in their dignity, than settlers from Europe and Asia. Yet it is only national identity, sense of belonging, representing and being represented by a given nation in Africa that can give one an African identity. Without such an identity it is not possible to have a Pan-African identity. Even the Black people of America who claim to have a Pan-African identity have it by proxy while their true identity is American. This does not mean that there is a limit to which human dignity can express and extend itself but that it has to have some concrete, spatial and historical manifestation in something that guarantees it security and ground to stand on. While somebody's dignity can be outstretched to cover the whole universe of beliefs; ideologies, concepts and nationalities without connection to a specific national identity such dignity remains nebulous. But the extension of national identity beyond nationality is essential to human dignity as long as this receives strengths and support from the national base.

Nobody can claim lack of responsibility for his country's national adventures, wars or sins and declare himself innocent before the victims of such adventures.

1.4 DIGNITY EXTENDS WITH FREEDOM AND RESPONSIBILITY

Human dignity starts always with freedom and ends with responsibility. If an African in Nairobi says something which offends or pleases a Chinese in Peking he is not free until he takes the blame or credit for the consequences. Dignity is the freedom by which a lover does not extend his love beyond activities for which he has no resources and capacity to cope with effects, both negative and positive.

16

Human dignity is more than good wishes, prayers, intentions and promises. It is risking to act on these and face the consequences. It is good to pray kneeling or sitting down only when you are going to stand up and go to do what you prayed for. Being a parent of a president is not the significant act until the children and citizen acknowledge that you are worthy dignity of your position. This is why a society should have constitutional, psychological or electoral method of checking that nobody gets contract or appointment for which he has no abilities to fulfil. For the same reason, the society should not award certificates, permits, licences, and duties to persons whose talents and resources are below what is required to succeed. Positions, ranks and roles are nothing but instruments of extending a person's dignity to others through service.

Dignity is the intimate responsibility in which one will account before God for his talents, if he fails to use them, and to society for their misuse. When this responsibility ceases due to sickness the society through friends or family takes over. The society must take care of its criminals in person or mentally sick in health facilities because these have wilfully or accidentally failed to be responsible for their existence and that of others. Infants must also be taken care of by responsible adults until they acquire responsible skills for their behaviour. At no time does a nation abdicate its responsibility for all its people both good and evil.

Even a Christian consciencious objecter who refues to participate in an unjust war waged by his country, does by his conscience continue to exercise a profound influence on the systems of law, religion and state by which he is governed. His anti-military conscience concretizes in a personal and individual manner his objection to any force or power that might want to set its own sovereignty above human dignity. The great nation-state with its claim for absolute power, and the modern science with its unprecedented analytic power cannot be as powerful or the human feelings, myths, illusions, visions, fictions, stories, dreams and aspirations whenever people are willing to act upon these and make them real in history. There is no state, science, technology or power in this world that can replace for ever the human desire for mercy, love, justice and respect. It is only these aspects of human dignity that give legitimacy and credibility to the existence of the ethics, laws, religion, politics and economics by which people continue to their own existence. The sovereignty of the individual is exercised by the state on his behalf but cannot be usurped by the state without the state destroying its own dignity and identity. While the state receives its identity and dignity from those it governs itself gives them none. It is their instrument of protecting their national identity and dignity.

There is great danger in allowing physical, material and legal institutions to outlive the transcendent and abstract dimension of their purpose of existence. No government, church or business should continue to live after having lost its spirit. In other words, people should not support the Sabbaths, customs, traditions and institutions that have lost touch with their original goals of existence. The instrinsic value of any social, economic, religious or political institutions is that it serves and fulfils human dignity. A good state is an instrument of justice in the hands of national dignity. Like salt which has lost its taste, a nation which loses its human dignity will be thrown away and be trodden down by those supposed to be its members. A good state is to the nation what a good deacon is to the church.

We have many examples of dignity being intimate freedom with responsibility. Daniel, Meshak and Abedinego never abdicated their freedom to choose life or death when the king of Babylon demanded that everybody should worship an idol. Elijah and Jeremiah knew the consequences of standing for their dignity when they challanged official idolatry of their times. Dedan Kimathi, the Freedom fighter, in whose name I dedicate the above argument, believed that dignity of his country was valuable enough to pay for it with his own life.

Dignity is to sacrosanct that it remains in the custody of the owner from birth to grave and continues in his name for days, years, decades and centuries after his earthly existence. The name of person stands for him and may continue to stand for him centuries after his bodily existence. The name of Jomo Kenyatta, Tom Mboya and J. M. Kariuki do have more influence and power in much of our present behaviour than of many of our present leaders. The name of a person may even stand for his power more effectively where he is not there than when he is. Jesus Disciples, Peter, James and John never performed the kind of miracles they performed in the name of Jesus of Nazareth when Jesus was alive. 1st Paul discovered that the name of Jesus is above every other name (Phil. 2:9-11) resisting and finally having been overcome by it.

Dignity confers itself to names, status, position, office, profession family, church or country and accept the blame and cost of what happens. The blame or responsibility for any office or institution always goes to the person who occupies it. There is no dignity in a king, pidge, priest, parent, captain or teacher who cannot accept personal responsibility per his office, role or inheritance. The Bible is against Adam shifting responsibility to his wife and his wife to the snake for his office as a leader in the garden of Eden. Never say, "it is the snake, devil, hunger, sickness, power, authourity or ignorance that made me eat the forbidden fruit."

A leader cannot hide behind the armophous, ambiguous and indifinite system when things go wrong. It was not possible for the lieutenant who ordered the My Lai massacres where Vietnamese children and grass were destroyed with napalm to abdicate responsibility for his grossly disproportionate use of fire power. The American soldiers were themselves completely demoralized and dehumanized by the behaviour of their officers who ordered them to do things which left them morally powerless. You cannot have moral power to do things morally powerless. You cannot have moral power while refusing responsibility for the negative effects of your actions. It is dignity that says, "I am sorry, forgive me, I am ready to pay for the consequences." It is being able to accept blame for the consequences of ones political, military, religious or conomic actions that distinguishes human beigs from animals. Animals may bite whatever threatens them; stones fall on miners who shake them and germs sicken a good man but these have no moral accountability. People should not act on impulse.

It is this freedom and responsibility of dignity that human institutions and nations represent and safe-guard. A nation or church is a person by extension because it receives its existence from those constituting it. The nation is the only institution of the world large and powerful enough to offer equal participation of dignity for all its members. All human beings are equal in dignity and unequal in vanity.

This leads us to point out that vanity is the fall of man from human dignity. I used to think of dignity as the ranks, positions, status and roles that special people occupied in society ad thought of chairman of co-operative societies, politicians, priests, bankers, chiefs, shopownersand polygamists as having more self-worth than other citizens. In my village, dignity was associated with the politicians, preachers and chiefs who called public meetings and then came two hours late in order for everybody to notice their arrival in their newly acquired motor cycles, bicycles and chrome plated cars. This dignity in the colonial fashion was nothing but vanity, oppression, snobbery, self-conceit and disregard for others. By the time I discovered that dignity cannot exist in the possessions of a person, I was a victim of thinking of cars, ranks, motorcycles, modern three piece suits as manifestations of dignity. When Christ came to my life I started noticing how knowledge, wealth and power can be used as instruments and extensions of vanity in people who profit and get credit without minding the negative consequences.

Vanity is therefore the antithesis of human dignity. It is the self-worship which results in the use of resources to force others to worship the self-worshipper. A man of vanity may use the national economy, politics, institutional structures and armed forces as his self-extension and then use them further to compel others to worship him. The idolatry of some people is so open that some kings in the Roman Empire used to set idols sculptured like them for public worships. Today's self-worshippers may not build physical idols, but they sculpture philosophies, ideologies, doctrines, parties, industries, churches and projects by their own image and require that everybody bows down to these. Vanity in a creed, beauty show, theory, policy, plan or ideal is no different from vanity carved into a piece of wood, stone or clay. Just as these idols have no noral feelings or perceptual responsibility to prayers, honour nd value given to them, their worshippers feel no moral obligations and responsibilities to the consequences of their power and influence in the world.

The people who worship their idols, thus, theories, dogmas, parties, armies, policies, laws, decrees, titles, popularity, fame and possessions, and carry out decisions based on obedience to these idols, are as dead in their conscience and lifeless in their feelings as the idols themselves. The image of man, fashioned, patterned and imitated from the images he himself has sculptured and moulded, by hands or brain, is petrified, callous, plastic and nechrophillic as the pieces of his labour. There is dignity in work, in creating and developing something, but not in allowing the product of your work to dictate what else you are going to be. The problem with populists is that they want to remain popular all their lives. This makes them slaves to other people's opinion about them. One must admit that he cannot run as fast as he used to do or is not as clever or rich as he used to be so that public opinion does not pierce him to become or remain a statue ad monument of his past glories.

Living under one's own vanity of pretending that one is King, rich, clever and powerful, while he is not, may be due to wanting to cling to some image of one-self one manufactured, produced, achieved, carved or was given in the past, or even expected to attain in the future but failed, but it shortcircuits the human emotions, frustrates and depresses them. It is a kind of homosexuality, or lesbianism, whereby creative energies meant for at giving pleasure to someone legitimate become misdirected and pervertedfrom their natural target and used for givig pleasure to oneself. Vanity is always possessive and exploitative because it cannot be satisfied with its culture, environment, history and personality. It is self destructive and without respect for anybody. All its machineries, money, sex, power and inventions are for making and acquiring more of them to fill its hollow and bottomless heart. Vanity is an exercise in futility. Vanity has no national culture, politics or identity because it exists by undermining these. It is a satan who makes hell for evrybody including himself.

In this sense, vain people have no true friends, families or nations because they see these as objects of helping them to make more, bigger and fancier idols, armies and bombs. The bigger the idol they create the more they become disatisfied with it. The greatest killer of great evangelistic, charismatic leaders, financial tycoons and mass media celebrities is vanity, when the original capactity to fascinate and pull large crowds of people dwindles. Some Kenyans parents force their children into mental break down trying to produce some scholars, celebrities, professionals and leaders out of them according to what they themselves had desired to become but failed. We cannot always remain at the top of power, wealth, knowledge and success. We should yield to younger and more dynamic leaders.

Prophets Isaiah and Elijah ridiculed the makers of idols and idol worshippers because idols symbolize and represent something accomplished, fixed and dead, in contrast to the living God, the creator in whose image people are made. There is nothing wrong making, carving or sculpturing a piece of stone, wood, philosophy or doctrine as long as once that work is complete you can use them as images of doing, demonstrating other things. It is in the making of things that humanity has dignity not in the things themselves. It is in eating, serving, healing, caring and living that we have satisfaction but not in the ownership and worship of what that action produces. We the humanity of today should guard against becoming shadows, portraits and statues of the governments, churches, economies and names that arise out of our activities in this world. "For what does it profit a man to have the whole world and lose his life."(Matthew 16:26). We should have abundant life, not abundant material objects. Material objects are there to meet human necessities.

There are many people who live like walking shadows of the books they have written, companies they have organized and governments they have formed. Others live like photo copies of their degrees, professional certificates, medals and bank accounts. Vanity reduces a person's dignity to a miserable shadow or copy of something he did or owns. It is an obsession wiht what we used to be, should be, or ought to be, but are not. A president, king orpriest should be able to retire from his office achievement, fame, position and role without feeling that this will depreciate his dignity or make him cease to be. The moment you look at your own photograph portrait hanging on the wall as more dignified representative of yourself than your own living personality, you are spiritually dead. Self-worship, which is what makes us worship statues, monuments and images of ourselves freezes our abilities and capacities to adjust and adapt to retiment, constitutional changes and rapid downward economic mobility. Idolatry is by virtue of being the worship of a lifeless, finished and fixed product, what makes the worshipper cold, sterile, infertile inflexible and impotent. Other than one's nation there is nothing else big enough by which man extends his dignity. Through the nation dignity fulfil itself without creating personality cults. When something by which we extend our dignity assumes independence from us and enslaves us to become extension of its power and influence we cease acting like human beings ad become like mechanical objects, merciless, passionless and loveless robots. It is no longer our will but of that institution, object or shadow that prevails once we fail in our human responsibiity for it. We should never allow the states, armies and churches which we create to extend our will and justice in the world to take over and to run that will and justice independently without reference to our present dignity. We must remain always and for ever responsible for the assignments we give to our social, political and economic agencies.

Most of what we call demonic, godless, devilish and evil powers are not angelic and heavenly forces intruding into our human affairs but the extension, influences and excesses of our own power in the hands of irresponsible agencies and agents. We blame governments for the wars, our taxes, votes and regligence, help to sustain. The final end of vanity is to annihilate, disseminate and kill human dignity. Nihilism, abyss, chaos and nothingness are the predestined end of vanity.

23

As a dignified child of God, I am a being whom I am irrespective of what I have, without regard to whether I win game trophies or war medals. I would do my best to express my dignity in competition with others who are trying to do the same as long as we agree that nobody becomes superior or inferior when one loses and the other wins. A Kenyan may rejoice for having won an Olympic medal, not because he has more dignity than the foreigners whom he has defeated but because this gives him opportunity to realize his God given talents. it is vanity that makes some Kenyan politician to celebrate their victory over others and then, later, appeal to them to bury their hatchets. They forget that hatchets exist in the hearts and minds of men who bury them and keep on digging them out to cut any throat of an opponent who might appear to rise up again. While competitive struggle is necessary to improve the quality and discipline of the servants of God in society, it becomes counter-productive when it destroys any of those involved in it.

Vanity is therefore the power directed at self-service at the expense of demeaning, reducing, de-humanizing, oppressing, exploiting competing or destroying others or their dignity. The power of vanity may not only cause loss of life itself, but may force, influence, compel, persuade, command, teach, push, confront, reduce, intoxicate, sedate, deceive, delude, dupe, lead, torture, threaten or aids its human victim to suffer and forfeit his self-respect, self-esteem, self-confidence, well-being, welfare, rights, and means of existence. Vanity may manifest its power visible as a witch, authority, institution, budget, dominion, office, idea, sexism, money or class. Vanity is a spiritual force of evil which may work through material and physical objects. Vanity may exist in a person who comes to us like a wolf in sheeps clothing. Social institutions must serve the national identity of the people or be abolished.

For this reason to allow any material, spiritual, physical or ideological institution to exist in society without it being an extension of national dignity is the worst from human irresponsibility. When institutions and their incumbents fall from national dignity, these become the instruments of sectarian vanity. Good judges, schools, churches, states, parliaments, chairmanships, presidencies **and armies** can easily turn into the instruments of local devils, **if allowed** to perpetuate themselves without accountability **to national** dignity. A beautiful country can become a harlot, **depraved,** unfaithful, mischevous, lunatic, cruel, immoral, **and** oppressive if allowed to fall from national dignity **as** Ugandans have experianced through many civil wars. **Vanity** is any power in wrong hands or surplus in the hands of a selfish group. Surplus power in the state or church is likely to be abused to undermine th legitimate national authority. Power is surplus when people not expected to exercise it pretend to exercise it on behalf of the legitimate rulers.

Nevertheless any power is evil power if exercised to divide people in order to make it possible for some to exploit others. When institutions, governments, junitas or leaders divide people in order to rule them, playing one people against another, they destroy their national identity. Some of the evil tactics may be so much institutionalized that the death, replacement or change of leaders does not make any essential differences. The whole work of evil may have to be destroyed like "Jesus came to destroy the work of the devil." 1 John 3:8.

There is only one condition of having institution and leaders, that is;they move to the same direction as all the people they are serving, they run toward a common goal. Leaders and institutions must follow the same purpose, goal and cause as their followers. A leader is a follower of the same constitution, laws, aspirations and aims as his followers and therefore their number one follower and servant.

The leader therefore receives from his supporters the mandate to become their voice, extension and dignity as long as he remains accountable to them. Leadership is therefore not abstract spiritual position that elevates leaders above followers, but a bodily, institutional and practical responsibility given to a follower by other followers. When Jesus saw that Peter was not willing to follow but only lead he told him, "get behind me Satan." Satan was dropped from heaven by God because he had selfish ambitions for leadership.He never wanted to follow and help other followers follow the same God faithfully.

25

Just as dignity is a power capable of self-extension through national institutions, vanity is also capable of ursurping national institutions for the purpose of self-extension. It can take over mass media, films, radio, books, magazines and pollution. Vanity in the hand of Hilter, worked in Germany the way apartheid ·in the hands of Vorster, Verwood and Botha, works in South Africa. But no matter how strongly vanity may appear to have prevailed over dignity, dignity repents its irresponsibility and rises from its fall with greater strength. Jesus Christ knew the power of dignity when he organized a small band of twelve disciples and charged them like salt or yeast. Dignity in the hearts of a few is more powerful than silver, gold and bombs in the hands of many. It becomes contageous and changes people to change things.

Once dignity is directed at the work of transforming society it becomes too powerful to reduce it to existing structures. It explodes mythologies, mysteries and fears about the power of vanity. It starts to encompass every new, creative and developing institutions as an alternative to the prevailing evil structures. If this were ot the case Kenya would never have gained independence and when independence came it would not have found new agents and actors to manage it. In fact, it was within the belly of colonial vanity of passbooks, "Kipande", and emergency laws that dignity selected its own agents. As a practical belief in the future dignity was able to produce people to rule that future. Dignity institutionalized itself in the roles, offices, positions and works of those engaged in the struggle for freedom and finally, replaced the old institutions. This means that dignity creates and develops its own institutional agents,ideas, theories and perceptions urging the process of practical struggle against vanity. A new national identity comes from dignity of a person who volunteers to die defending his country and fighting to liberate it from the vanity of any illegitimate power, or order or regime.

Sometimes the power of dignity may not be as much present in a prince, king, civil servant or politician as it is in the victims of present economic, politics and religion. Dignity may not manifest itself among the oppressed as' was the case with Israelite in Egypt before God intervened through Moses to free them. It was in the process of Exodus, in their journey to Cannan, that the Israelites obtained the salvation of their national dignity. Hence, dignity may depart from thrones, chairs, parliaments, courts and laws and get lost completely until recovered through a journey to self-discovery. This is why I like pursuing metaphysical, supernatural and abstract ideas because in this process they become real in my life. But the final origin and source of dignity is not metaphysical or supernatural ideas by myself in whom dignity awakens the image of God. Similarly the final and original source of the dignity and identity of a nation is not the national institutions, state, governments, churches, schools, courts, policies, laws, customs or traditions, but the people in whom these may awaken the sense of self-worth and from whom national dignity may be derived. This makes it absolutely necessary to fight vanity not by vanity, but by awakening in humanity the original purpose and essence of being human. Thus to "Love your neighbour as yourself."

This love component of human dignity can be extended to institutions as justice. No institution can practise independently without this human factor of dignity. National identity depends on national dignity. As long as people themselves never abandon their responsibility for love to the institution they can use the institution to help them share love with one another.

In other words, voters should not abdicate their dignity to the people they elect into power positions in committees, parliaments, councils and cabinets, because delegation of power is never abandoment of responsibility. The public which pays taxes and elects leaders to maintain national social political, economic and religions structures, is ultimately responsible for the behaviour and action of those running those structures. The people must always reserve the right to hire and fire their agents, actors and representatives. In Kenya, the president removed some land buying companies because they had become instruments of vanity in the hands of greedy men. When the power of vanity is so overwhelming that the institutions it occupies are too. dependent on it to

27

become free, then those institutions have outlived their usefulness. When a man loses responsibility to his habits of spending drinking, eating, the best way to save his is to abolish the system in which his drinking, eating or spending is his master. This is the kind of masterdom of evil which made people irresponsible by making them backslide from Christian faith. Paul described this evil and overwhelming influence of ones habit, customs and traditions as principalities and powers. Rom. 8:38 - 39.

There are times when one cannot tell whether dignity is in an office, officer or structure or in all of them. Is the dignity of a good school in the staff and students, the school structure or the whole school? Is the dignity of Kenya in the people, the government or the social organization? Sometimes we think of the institutional structure of Kenya Police as the best in the world. The fact that it has a few corrupt policemen who demand bribes does not worry us. But no matter how righteous individuals working for the colonial government used to be, no Mau Mau freedom fighter would have consider him so. This means that people distinguish between a righteous system employing crooks from a wicked system employing righteous individuals, but at the same time holding the righteous individuals accountable and responsible for their employment in a wicked system. A righteous man working as an agent or proxy of evil due to ignorance is still liable punishment. One cannot serve two masters, "God and mammons," Jesus said.

There used to be a time when most Kenyans held evil spirits, magical spells, witchcraft and mystical objects as the agents of evil that threatened human dignity with curses, diseases and calamities. Now they think of the Atomic bombs and other incomprehensible means of destruction as playing the same role of opposition to dignity as those ancient supernatural forces. So our question is not whether vanity occupies a heavenly or earthly, superstitious or scientific, or religious or material object, but that from whatever its source and through whichever agent it comes, it is our enemy.

If I have dignity at all, then I have freedom and responsibility to say yes or no to the influence, powers, forces and temptations that require my co-operation. Dignity is my free choice to be myself without assistance from God or man. This freedom is absolute, inalienable, and without compromise because I may choose to retain or abandon it. Dignity is choice between life and death, heaven and hell, grace and condemnation. Only dignity can freely declare "Give me life or give me death." Only a person, church or government that has dignity can recognize dignity in others because it knows the smell, language, cry, image and value of dignity from its own. God recognizes our dignity because he has his own dignity or divinity. Dignity recognizes itself everywhere and in everybody wherever it exists. While the vanity of a master produces as slave, the dignity of a person produces another tree one like him. In his own likeness God created us as his friends. But evil is in and tension with anything good and therefore cannot recognize or create dignity.

Even when evil likes evil, it is because it can use it as a means to its own end. Thieves, gangsters and mafia cannot free themselves from the others without risking destruction. But when man rebels from God, God sacrifices his own son to save and redeem him. To belong to vanity is to lose not only dignity but freedom and responsibility. The fact that tribes, clans and sectional groups have the tendency to act like gangsters when it comes to sharing of national resources with others justifies their abolition and replacement by national identity. Ethnic identities may continue to function in Kenya for centuries to come but not as national structures with institutional authority to allocate power, positions, resources and other means of existence. While these may not be instrinsically evil, tribal systems can be easily manipulated by leaders willing to make tribalism out of tribes. Dignity requires its own institutional forms of love, justice and service in organizations that do not exclude anybody on the basis of tribe, race, religion or origin.

National identity represents human dignity when the nation depends upon its people for its essence and existence. The term people is always positive, rspectable, invaluable and Godly. If it is the people who endow the nation with its identity, then national identity and human dignity mean one and the same thing. But if the nation derives its dignity from elsewhere for instance from its parties, leaders, institutions, philosophies, policies, constitutions or traditions, it may become alientated from people's identity, may be one and the same phenomenon at one time, but become two different things like Kenyans and Kenya government during colonial times. The Kenya national identity represented not the people but the policies, ideologies, economics and politics of the British colonial system. It is the duty and responsibility of the people to make sure that their identity and that of their nation will never become two separate entities of existence, but will remain one category of national existence with human essence. Any separation of human dignity and national identity makes the two forces negative and antagonistic to each other.

Nations depend for their existence on people and people are the essence of nations. While systems of power like Apartheid and Nazism may displace the people as the essence that gives a nation its existence people remain always the higher principle of national conflict. Sooner or later they discover that something in their nation has usurped their national dignity. The people as a whole cannot have vanity. Only some of them trying to exploit and take advantage of others can have vanity. The Bible confirms the idea of the people as the bearers of God's mercy. In Israel God sided with the poor and oppressed. In God's judgement, people out-rank any individual in their holiness, perfection and value.

Human dignity cannot therefore be lost in everybody in any nation. Even in Sodom and Gomorah there was somebody who God found righteous. It is for the sake of remnant of dignity that when the nation loses dignity and assumes vanity that God awakens a few prophets to revive dignity in everybody. Prophets help those who have lost dignity and give it only lip service to change and be saved. This salvation may call for the rebuking of any of the systems of power that destroy human dignity. It awakens them to realize that dignity exists not in armaments and gold but in people.

At one time, my three year old child thought that human dignity consisted in smoking but wondered why I did not smoke. He started to pretend that he is smoking by taking a piece of firewood with the far end ignited into his mouth. When I saw this I tore a big piece of news paper and rolled it into something like a cigarrette. I lighted one end and asked him to put the other end in the mouth to inhale the smoke. He started complaining and crying saying that what he wanted was the right smoke, not something to smoke. Freedom to smoke or not smoke, and not the fact that he was the son of a clergyman was what he wanted. He wanted to know whether his dad who does not smoke had as much dignity as smokers. But instead of explaining this to him I gave him something that he described as poison in his mouth. It is at this point that he disclosed to me that he wondered why his dad did not smoke, which means he had doubts about his thought of dignity in smoking.

Dignity is possessions, properties, degrees, positional and status exists as long as we think these have dignity. But nobody can deny that the possession of food, clothes and shelter is not a part of our dignity. Hungry people may become so desparate that they start eating one another like cannibals. Their cannibalism has the same effect as the cruelty and injustice of the leaders who sell food to earn foreign cash for buying cars. Malicious aggression is always evil when directed against oneself or against others, by suicide, cannibalism or by selling food to deprive the poor. A victim of aggression may have the choice to die of hunger or by being shot rioting for food, by electrocution or hanging, but all the same he has lost his dignity.

In all cases and all circumstances human dignity is not likened to the physical body but expresses itself through work, agents, institutions but cannot be found elsewhere when it ceases to exist in the actual existing and living person. My identity, credit or social security card, owes it value to my dignity. If I steal a drivers licence, credit card or money, the people who discovered that these are stolen will see them as symbols of my vanity. It is my "ontological existence," i.e. existence which shows that how I appear, look or seem is true

31

and authentic, that give credibility to what I say, possess or do.

Absolutely, nothing has value in this world except by the virtue of people thinking and apreciating it has value. Cultures, civilisations, knowledge, history and science are ways of evaluating and classifying the value of things according to their use by men. ..Just as my car cannot dictate where I must go and food cannot tell me when to eat it, nothing should have power to dictate to me my worth. All values to which the nation is the chief value and for which I must voluntarily sacrifice myself to defend derive from the act that they are values from me. That to which I am totally committed and involved, like my Church and my Country, even my family is something I can die defending it because its existence reflects my own existence and projects it to a greater future than I can project by myself. When one says "There is no government without representation," in this statement, he is saying that I can die creating one which represents me. This representation of my dignity is so dynamic that it can exist in another person. If I feel that the leader of my church or my president is the one who at this time speaks the truth and automatically sums up the reasons I want live, I may defend him with my life. There exists no material things that can represent my dignity and make me feel more dignified like ideas of justice or truth. There were many prophets of God who accepted persecution because they believed in justice and truth. The justice and truth for which they died was in their hearts but expressed in ideas. Similarly the country, president, church leader, friend or family that a person may die for is not necessarily the one physically observable, but the essence and value in his position. So, in fact, he gives his life for that which has given him his life. This is why Paul and other christians found no difficulties preferring to follow Christ through life or death. No wonder some people may chose death in dignity defending economic and political institutions whose dignity is their dignity, of creating a national culture with values consistent in national dignity. Without a national culture nationalism would intesify tribal differences. Education is the most effective tool of abolishing indifference and ignorance that perpetuate vain self-interest. The prophet Isaiah heard the word of God saying, "My people are destroyed for lack of knowledge; because you have rejected knowledge, I reject you from being my priest."

There is no dignity in national institutions without local institutions that *feel* see and hear dignity in the individual life and activities. National identity without town, village and city dignity to constitute may be too abstract for many people. Apart of the nation must be in the hands of everyone through mediation by families and locally based institutions other than the tribe or clan. National identity must be accessible, accountable and available where people are, as farmers, nomads, villagers or families. Families are the basic institutions of survival because they own shelter, food and means of production such as land, skills and tools. They are the institutions of human self-reproduction, sexual satisfaction, nursing care and security of old age. The central government institution may be replaced by new and different ones but families are irresplaceble and lack any known substitute. This means that dignity is synonymous with national identity based on participation in meaningful human relationships such as children enjoying in their families.

When Kenyans devote themselves to religion, they do so not as idle pastime but because religion transforms them from isolationism, individualism and nationalism toward a national identity which can accommodate and appreaciate (gnity from people, other nations and cultures. Even our people, other nations and cultures. Even our beggars in Nairobi do believe that religion translates their dignity into universal dignity which makes visitors from other countries throw coins into thier alms trays. In this sense religious beliefs concretize themselves into national identity when a Kenyan beggar thinks that foreigners find the image of God in him when they come to visit his country. But I have no doubt that the dignity of a beggar is below national standard of national identity and beggars should be stopped from their sub-human existence.

In my recent research amongst members of my Church and teachers I discovered that many of them measure their dignity with the amount of time they spend doing something. Most of the teachers I interviewed equate dignity with the hours one spends in school, at the church or at home. If one spent more hours in these three institutions he was supposed to have more dignity than the one who spent more time in sports, clubs or bars. Others felt that dignity is equal the amount of money one is willing to spend on something. If one spent more money on housing, education and feeding the family he was supposed to have more dignity than the one who spent more in cigarrettes, beer, leisure and prostitution than other things. So the amount of resources of time and money one is willing to spend on one thing is preference to another may reflect dignity or vanity. Time and money spent on pleasing others, the teachers said, proved dignity and spent on oneself selfishly, vanity. As more and advertisement in the mass media is allowed for things spent on vanity the values of our society may change and weaken the present level of moral dignity.

It is interesting how these teachers preferred to spend their lives as teachers with low pay and little prospects of promotion because that gave them dignity. Parents described themselves as dignified by their fatherly and motherly work because it gives them opportunity to share their lives with someone else. This is why they spend every moment and money available to promote the wellbeing of their off-spring from whom they expect no pay or reward. It is a dignifying thing to create someone else in your own likeness and see your dignity produce dignity. When they see children grow and become adults like them they hear an inner voice of dignity telling them "well done".

Therefore, people who let opporunities of serving others pass by will go to hell where someone will force them to pay for the service they received from others by working for nothing. God's image, that is, his dignity in us, exists in our lives as long as we remain creative like him by creating institutions for the furtherance and extension of dignity. It was due to the majesty and dignity of God as the creator that he never wanted to abandon his work in vain when Adam sinned but sent a new dignity to man in Jesus Christ is our dignity. We dignify from him by participating in his work or reforming, transforming, improving, reconciling and saving the world. This means creating a world order consistent with the kingdom of God. As long as we institute love and justice in the family and nation this proves that we are the children of God called Kenyans or other nationals. If I am not a child of God as a Kenyan I cannot know an Israelite, Briton, Russian, Indian or Papuan can be a child of God. God himself became real in the world through incarnation in Judah, in Israel, during the times of Herod and Pilate. In our own time our dignity must be in flesh and bones in order to suffer and die for that which is spiritual and eternal. There are times when foreign religion like christianity and Islam may have a conflict with our national dignity by laying emphasis on foreign history, culture and language.

Justice as the dignity of a worm is in order to grow big and become a beautiful butterfly, the dignity of any individual is national in order to grow mature, rich, educated and powerful so that it can become universal. Power, wealth and knowledge are like leaves that a human catapillar must eat to achieve a full national identity, so that he can metamorphosis to become free to fly into freedom. If a catapillar eats leaves to fatten itself and remain a worm it will become like churches and governments which become big and mighty and collapse on their own weight. The purpose of any institution to tax its people is for gaining ability to transcend its own need to grow big in order to serve the people. Institutions are mere instruments of extending and sustaining human dignity.

In the next eight chapters we shall devote much time examining the practical operations of dignity in orderly development and humanization of the systems by which human beings continue their existence.

CHAPTER 2
THE POWER AND INFLUENCE OF HUMAN DIGNITY

How much we think we are worth has a powerful influence on how much we make our country to be worth. It is our dignity that motivates us to build and construct our nation to be a true reflection of who we are, to mirror our likeness. Dignity alone has power to prevent the corruption of our national identity by militarism, materialism and rivalry. The inner power of dignity reflects itself externally as social justice, minding of other's welfare, peace, respect, love and unity.

Without this powerful influence of human dignity in social, economic and political relations we cannot achieve the necessary moral motivation to work together for national goals, harmony in the family, national unity, peace with our neighbours and respect for life. As long as people share a common national identity rooted in their human dignity, this motivates them to serve the country without the lust for immediate material wealth and positions. Without a strong national identity based on human dignity policemen and other armed forces may be tempted to think of their profession as something extra over and above human dignity. It is dignity that calls all worldly powers to their instituted purpose and makes each member of a social system, whether a soldier, teacher, doctor or preacher think of himself not more highly than others.

Failure to achieve economic development is not what leads to political chaos and social disintegration but the loss of human dignity in human expectations. There used to exist some follacy that if the armed forces were paid higher salaries than civilians they would never be tempted to take over power or accept bribery. But soldiers become deliquent for the same reason doctors, lawyers, shopkeepers and manufacturers price their services and commodities above the ability of ordinary people to afford. When people cannot share their skills and resources on the basis of national dignity, but only on the basis of profits, they become enemies. This leads to strikes, riots, revolts and rebellions because some people feel their dignity as being slighted by others. If sweepers, cooks and housewives are given the right recognition as human beings they will not flee away from their homes and country.

The same power of dignity that influenced people to serve the country in the struggle for independence, without pay, endures and survives as a national ethic whenever people are called to serve the country, as in the case with harambee movement. It is when people are under-paid in order for greedy companies and employers to make huge profits that the spirit of service conflicts with that of exploitation. The visible power of dignity takes the form of resistance to exploitation in order to create equitable and just distribution of resources. The power of human dignity works against overwhelming forces of evil as proven by the self-sacrifice of those who follow patterns of life Christ exhibited on the cross.

Dignity works more by influence than by mechanical force. Unlike the power of manipulation, gun or physical blow, the power of dignity is like that of the sun which makes plants grow by its creative influence. This power of dignity is what connects the power of money to make more money into the power of money for meeting human needs. Dignity connects the office of a bishop, president, general or corporate director into the power of caring, reason, love and compassion. It is this power behind human compassion and forgiveness, and not money and arms that make the nation great. The power of human dignity is above the power of political self-interests and self-preservation. It is this power to give ones life for the nation, or others, that the Jewish and Roman authorities recognized in Jesus, when they mocked him saying, "You saved others, save yourself." But Jesus' power of dignity was not for self-salvation but for national salvation, for the building of God's kingdom. When I think of God's kingdom, I do not think of it as some spiritual realm in the air, but as some concrete reality with earthly manifestation in my country through the state and other institutions.

Other forms of power, when acting independently of human dignity and outside of national identity, become expressions of self-interests, and may pursue self-salvation at the expense of common salvation.

Only when self expresses itself through love, sharing, compassion, peace, justice and respect for others that it becomes emancipated from selfishness and finds fulfilment from beyond itself, from others. Self is always destructive of itself and other selves unless it ceases being devoted to self-service and becomes devoted to the services of others. Therefore self is a positive force when it seeks peace with others and is a source of creative power when it finds satisfaction in actions that satisfy others. When this positive, creative and independent power in our minds releases enough psychic and spiritual resources and forces to overcome the selfish, satanic and demonic tendencies within us, we become healthy personalities and citizens capable of building a healthy nation.

However, the power of dignity may use negative power to negate evil powers. Dignity can apply force if necessary but itself is not forceful. Law and grace must work side by side with each other in a world where some men have lost their conscience. It is like the power of the father which applies love to make the child understand things while at the same time using the cane when necessary to drive the message of love right into the head of the child. Even God, in Christ works in our minds as a positive power which becomes negative toward sin and other forms of evil. Where dignity exists God is present and his spirit at work to overthrow and punish workers of evil.

World history is full of instances in which human dignity would not have achieved anything without using revolutions as clubs to drive home into the hearts of oppressive regimes the gospel of justice. Sir William Wilberforce and his Clapham Sect influenced the British government to mobilize the navy to put an end to slave trade and slavery.

Some of human dignity is useless unless put into effect through institutional organisations such as the state, church or school. While every person has the right to claim dignity as his authority of being a child of God, it does not help anyone to have such an authority of being a child of God, it does not help anyone to have such an authority unless he can translate it into the rights for sharing world's resources and spiritual blessings. Even such platitudes as life, liberty and property do not mean anything unless those entitled to them do have control over the means of existence. This is why the state is a human equipment to help people achieve greater heights of dignity by guaranteeing them access to the basic means of survival. Just as a human being has hands to do things for himself, the nation has the state to do things for itself. The various ministries of the government are like state fingers to hold various instruments of service like education, medicine or food.

Hence, in order to survive, dignity seeks unity and harmony with everything in the environment, family, community and nation. It exerts itself as power and influence. So, dignity never rests until it manifests itself in all human and national activities. The nation takes care of all its people like a person takes care of himself. What a man does to his own body with his hands the nation does to itself by use of state institutions.

Any weakness in dignity would, in Kenya, bring ethnic conflicts because the organs of the government would appear like tribal rather than national hands. The energies necessary for constructive development would be spent on imaginary conflicts. A person without faith in national identity becomes not only envious of other's success but becomes a thief, oppressor, criminal and rumour-mongerer to spoil it.

Life without dignity does not only pose infections, dangers, to the dignity of others in society but also alienates itself from self, community and God. The greatest form of alienation is the loss of ones' national identity. A man without national identity may think of himself as inferior or superior to others. Superiority complex may lead to self-worship. This self-worship alienates others by its obnoxious demands, self-conceited arrogance, and abnormal showing off. Hitler and Amin did not only have tendencies to self-worship but required that other human beings be sacrifised to their power. They suffered from the egocentric complex in which lack of human dignity leads people to think of themselves as the centre of the world and others as animals for sacrifice. People who think of themselves as having a better identity than the national identity do create personality cults around their names in which national identity becomes confused with cultic worship. There is a big problem in the world of how to detect a heartless, profane and demonic man before he arises to political or military power. A man without soul can pretend to be the most holy and loving in order to win mass support from democratic and peace loving people. After winning the power he imposes himself upon them as their god.

He can exploit the plight of the people and use nationalism as a stepping stone toward self-enthronement as Satan. In contrast to the self-sacrificial power of dignity the power of such a vain and selfish leader is gained and preserved through deception, intrigue, treachery, and pretnce. Unlike the freedom fighters who shed their blood for the country such treacherous power-mongers bank their money in foreign countries out of fearing what will happen when their evils reveal their works of darkness. Their works of indignity prove that they do not trust the dignity of the national population which gave them their existence. Having lost loyalty to the population which animated, legitimated and gave it its power the leadership may perpetuate itself only as a manifestation of evil.

We have cases in which the central government in Kenya has intervened in Kiambu County Council and Nairobi Municipal Council to save people from the opportunists who had infiltrated their local governments and caused the breakdown of essential services. Not everybody in these councils was vicious and opportunistic but a few of the Christians there seemed not to have their behaviour touched by the blood of Christ. They had won voters support because they had pretended to be righteous. Those in the Nairobi City Council had swayed the electors by singing how Nairobi "is the crown jewel, the fair lady and the golden city in the sun". But no city can be golden in the sun unless its people are golden in their hearts. It is from our hearts that power is shaped and produced, and determined to be righteous or demonic.

Anybody who speaks of Nairobi as the crown of glory for Africa, the most lovely city in the world, automatically appeals to the sentiments of Kenyan dignity. Any mention of

Nairobi as a virgin bride adorned for her visitors and dwellers reminds people of Nairobi University, airports, libraries, museums, Bomas of Kenya, animals' orphanage, state house, headquarters of all ministries, beautiful streets, churches, temples, mosques, theatres, and hospitals. If you turn the hearts of Kenyans inside out you can find the real origin of every external and physical structures. Having elected into power those who have set the glory of Nairobi above the glory of all cities in the world the people feel disappointed and betrayed beyond measure when their councillors let the city in the sun run into the city under garbage and filth, to see classrooms turn into toilets and hotels turn into rat and fly breeding grounds. When the nomads, farmers, camel-riders and peasants of Kenya hear the *Voice of Kenya* speaking suspension of the City Council and its replacement by a commission then the crown jewel of their country loses its value in their minds. They hear of vanity, iniquity and corruption in the city and doubt the dignity of those the civilized urban dwellers had chosen to represent them. They conclude that the camel-rider has dignity and the car driver vanity.

Why do political criminals get away with it in a country where poor men selling fruits without licence can go to prison? How come that men striving for survival can be punished by those striving for power? Is dignity in conflict with power? The greatest temptation in life is to reward criminals who succeed into power and become wealthy and to punish the righteous who work hard and fail to gain power and wealth. For this reason men who should be in prison become the ones running our churches, councils, schools nd other institutions while those who make mistakes seeking something to sustain life go to prisons. The fact that good laws issue out of human dignity, does not mean that human vanity cannot disguise itself as government, church or business and use these laws as instruments of its evil ends. We have to recognize this human weakness to avoid its influence.

Human dignity is the essence of things functioning properly as intended by their creator. If God created men to live, even breaking the Sabbath to save life, is an expression of dignity.

When men rebel against colonial laws that confine them to slavery, as Kenyans did, they are obeying higher laws of dignity. For this reason unjust laws that violate or suppress activities for the fulfillment of dignity should be done away with. For instance, it is due to instincts of dignity that a person builds his shelter of cartons at a street corner rather than spend his rights in open space. When laws are used to justify the arrest, harassment and imprisonment of such a poor person they cease being instruments of the human dignity from which they issued and become instruments of vain men protecting their selfish interests.

The power of dignity derives from faith and conviction that what we do to sustain ourselves alive as an inseprable part of our dignity. One's initiative to determine one's own destiny is essential to being human. This autonomous character of human dignity makes people to determine themselves by how they earn their means of existence. An adult who depends on others to determine his life, to house, feed and clothe him is no different from pet animals.

Dignity therefore exists in us in so far as we are able to determine our own lives. This independence, self-reliance and freedom is necessary for community and national existence. Without such autonomous freedom men would lose their dignity to the state, church and family and make social existence destructive of human conscience. People cannot have fellowship with one another or love one another unless and until their personal identity is recognised and preserved by an independent nation from which issues the overt and external institutions, governments, churches, markets, hospitals and schools over which they have influence and control.

We share our grief, sorrow and misfortune only with those that recognize these as our common problems. St. Paul was able to convert the household of Caeser while he was imprisoned there because he was able to share his dignity with them. His sorrow and joy, pain and pleasure, and despair and hope permeated his captors who felt human like him. Any single Kenyan who has solved his personal problems has solved national problems

The dignity of Christ was in his willingness to share his divinity with mankind, and in that process suffered and died on the cross to redeem mankind. In St. Paul's theology death means the total destruction of the old sinful nature which Jesus Christ was willing to share on behalf of mankind and resurrection means the birth of the new life. It means transformation from being self-centred, opportunistic and egocentric. Loving and doing things for others, "love your neighbour as yourself" is the work in which dignity fulfills itself. Dignity is betrayed and destroyed by self-love.

Social systems as well as the church have no right to exist except in so far as they express human love and project human dignity. As instruments and expression of human dignity social structures, even the state, lose their right to exist when they start existing for themselves. Just as dignity does not exist for itself but for others any institution organised to serve human dignity loses its legitimacy and character if it outlives its dignity and starts serving itself. Just as a man who serves himself loses dignity, an institution which serves itself has outlived its usefulness. Self-service is the most sinister and demonic power in the world and must be broken, shattered and destroyed by the forces of human dignity. This is the point at which revolts and revolutions become instruments of God to help a country get rid of parasitical authorities. An authority of any kind whether of the church or state becomes false and tyrannical when it outlives its usefulness as a servant and becomes the tool of one class or group for exploiting another. All authority or power to rule, order and legislate must always remain the means of serving the population that constitute the nation.

Dignity and service go together in personality like two sides of the same coin. Because God created man with this attribute of service to one another any man or any human institution not having this attribute loses its blessings from God. To forsake service to one another is tantamount to challenging the creator. Just as the creator did not create himself but others, we become like him serving others. This service is always service to the nation whether it is ourselves, our

43

families or others across the country who benefit. Benefit to our country is benefit to ourselves. This humanity of God is what Jesus was expressing when he said, I was hungry, thirst and in prison but you did not help me. So, do not ask what your country can do for you, but what you can do for your country.

Our humanity must not lose its divinity if at all it must retain dignity. There is no point individuals acting as righteousness when they act as employers, employees, policemen, executives or auctioneers. We cannot depersonalize our institutions without causing them to be our instruments for self-destruction. What we cannot do personally as men and women, we should not do as chiefs, presidents, or generals. Institutions do, in fact, represent our corporate identity whether these are family, business, political, educational or national institutions. And since corporate identity as nations or churches represents our personal identity, we should abolish those corporate identities that have ceased to represent what we are, our dignity.

Even our faith in any state should always be subject to evaluation to see whether it continues to manifest faith in ourselves. We should always have faith in ourselves as children of God and not as products of man-made institutions. Our faith in any state should therefore be democratic questioning, analytical, critical and active so that the state makes sure to represent our interests and never its own. The state owes its existence to us while we do not owe ours to it. No government has any right to exist except as divine and human instrument for development, law, order and justice. Even the head of state owes loyalty to the nation whose people owe him loyalty corporately and individually.

If any state were to compete with its people for survival, thus wishing to survive at their expense, it would cease functioning according to its nature. *Man is the creator, originator, bearer, initiator and organizer of the state, is its god and therefore man must resist being a worshipper of his own creature.* The state cannot give man the right to worship his god because *man started worshipping God his creator long before he decided to create the state. Man is made by God to serve his purposes in the same way the state is made by man to serve his purpose.* The function of the state may be to protect man from any interference with his worship of God but the right to worship comes from the God who is being worshipped.

The state is therefore a human devise which can be used for good or for bad. Most Africans do acknowledge that General Amin used the state for bad. The state is a man-made institution dedicated to the service of humanity but which some wicked dictators can use for destroying humanity. This is why those in state authority must have their dignity checked, scrutinised and tested before being allowed to hold state positions. Dignity should be the criterion by which we measure the qualifications of those entrusted with the preservation of peace, law and order. Leaders of the state owe their dignity from the dignity of their people and retain that dignity as long as they defend the dignity of their people.

The state-should therefore preserve itself by preserving the rights of the individuals who created it. Law and order are the moral conditions through which human dignity is preserved but not the justification to use violence and eliminate opponents. If a national state violates or deliberately allows the violation of human rights it loses its constitutional legitimacy and political support. Like salt that has lost its taste it must be cast away to be trodden by men in their struggle to keep their sanity. Men cannot be sane without dignity. Once any institution violates human dignity it violates its own right to exist. South Africa is a case in point where the states policy of separate white-black development violates human dignity and invalidates its right to survive. The respect, esteem and faith people owe their head of state is that which they elected him to defend. A leader plants loyalty in the people by being loyal to them in order to harvest loyalty. God took action against the state of Israel when it alienated itself from God and the people. God had created the people and the people created the state. While the people may have created a government stronger than themselves God never created something stronger than himself. God always intervenes when men and women create a power stronger than their dignity and become unable to correct, restrain or prevent it from violating their rights. God punishes them by letting them suffer the consequences of having absolutized their own power and idolozing their leaders. Absolute power and idolatry constitute gross violations of national identity.

Hence, the power of our human dignity must never yield to the formation of powers that violate our national identity as righteous, just, loving, respectful and godly people. The identity of the state and its rulers must always reflect the needs and problems of the whole population, not simply those of the individuals in power. The identity of the state is subject to national identity. The state though the only national institution with a monopoly of political power, it should protect and respect other institutions that deal with religion or commerce.

It appears that some rulers of Africa portray an inferior quality of dignity compared with the dignity of those they rule. This is true especially when they keep on importing big cars for themselves while their people are crying for seeds to plant after long periods of draught. Do they owe their dignity from big gadgets or from their people? Why not silence the hungry with food rather than with the guns? But instead of providing seeds they provide their soldiers with more bullets to quieten the cries of the poor. Kenya is ahead of most countries of the world in spending more resources on the welfare of the people than on military and other state institution.

From this we deduce that good servants of the people are also good servants of God. Any state that pleases the population pleases its creators. A good head of state is the one who gives thanks to the population which created the state as its own instrument for self-preservation and sacrifises his life for them. Such a head of state reveals his nature as a wonderful example of the dignity of the population that gives him the authority to govern. The call to govern emanates from dignity and is the consequence of recognising divinity in all humanity.

Our dignity is so much dependent on the state for protection that the primary task of development in Africa is the development of the state itself, thus, the government, its institutions and personnel. The state that fails to pay attention to itself as the custodian of human dignity fails to distinguish itself from commercial institutions and becomes like another company which benefits only its owners. When rulers of Israel disobeyed God they started selling people for money and goods. Their nationals plans, policies and programmes were for taking more foreign wives and mortgaging their people for foreign goods. A pagan king like Cyrus of Persia who had no conscious plan to obey God was counted as having obeyed God when he redeemed the Israelites from their Babylon captivity. God never allowed kings to assume powers, indulgencies and pleasures that made them forget that power belongs to the people.

It is not that whatever the state does it must be always conscious of human dignity but that it must be always aware of the people as the creators of the state. The state is privileged to exercise moral values that individuals cannot exercise on their own such as the just distribution of resources, community peace and institutional orders.

On the whole, whether human dignity expresses through the power of the state and other institutions or through personality, it enjoys a lot of freedom in its activities. Its freedom is actualized through prophetic actions of love, peace, justice, compassion and mercy.

The products of dignity are not wealth, goods and services but order, unity, respect, confidence and esteem. When I was about sixteen years I discovered that in me there was something greater than in the boys from famous and rich families which attracted boys and girls to me. I discovered that my life as a motherless boy made me look to the community as my mother. To get what I wanted from the community I practised love, respect and esteem toward all its members adults and children alike. As a result of this attitude toward my community almost all members of the community adopted the same attitude toward me. I was therefore regarded like a son of every mother or father in my community. Everything in heaven and on earth became a part of the love, peace and justice that I received. I started seeing Jesus Christ as the centre of that world that I received. I started seeing Jesus Christ as the centre of that world in my community and until now I see Him as the centre of all communities.

Others may not see Christ as the centre of their world. Such people may tend to take certain ideology, phylosophy, creed or career as the centre of their dignity. There is nothing wrong with having economic plans, policies and programmes based on personal ideology or principle. Even such a general statement as development to uplift the living conditions of the people has the power of dignity behind it. A businessman indirectly serves the interests of his employees and helps them to enjoy work as a necessary exercise of dignity. A sportsman may derive his strength to pursue dignity in his victories. A soldier may see bravery as the focus of his dignity. Recently, I observed a *moran* selling cattle at a local market. Somebody quoted half the price than the *moran* was selling one of the cattle. The *moran* got infuriated by this and said "I won't mind killing you and getting hanged under the law. The only fear I have is breaking the law fighting a woman or killing a cow." For this *moran*, courage in fighting other men was the centre of his dignity. Our task is not to destroy but to transform the courage of such a *moran* into national dignity.

While Christ is the centre of my dignity, loyalty to my country and love for its people are the concrete expressions of that dignity. Just as the dignity of Christ resides in his incarnation, death and resurrection, and in his continuing work as redeemer and creator our dignity needs such concrete actions. It is as workers, teachers, ministers and parents in their labour to nurture, feed and educate the future generations that Kenyans exercise their living and dynamic qualities of dignity, thus, continuity and creativity. As human beings Kenyans must sustain themselves in values that outlive their biological existence and help the coming generations in doing the same.

Dignity without works is dead. We shall know dignity by its fruits. The tragedy of our country is that we elect and employ people into high positions of leadership on academic, professional and other merits without going into their faith in human worth.

Before appointing people into responsible positions they should be tested whether they have a philosophy of human dignity based upon social justice and a history of their own involvement in national service. Those whose experience in communal service is too limited to influence their decisions in the interests of the people should first join some kind of national service and have first hand experience in human hardships.

It is timely for Africans to have their dignity shaped in the crucible of real life outside the classrooms and offices. Even the highest ranking civil servants magistrates, administrators and technicians should be required to have months of field experience away from their offices after every several years of service. Every promotion should be accompanied with field experience and written report to prove that one is in touch with the people out there. Unlike things in science, technology and mathematics we cannot read from imported materials, that dignity is developed in the struggle for survival as individuals join hands to work together for their common destiny.

Dignity therefore has a lot to do to influence and become influenced by others in the context of their needs and problems. Otherwise lack of dignity as a positive influence will cause civil conflicts, refugee problems, and discrimination on the basis of race or tribe. The lack of dignity as a moral influence is at work in those leaders, who lacking patience love and respect of life resort to actions that distabilize the community, alienating others to say "if this country does not belong to all of us, it belongs to nobody."

In conclusion, we have seen that dignity has power and influence over human behaviour and institutions. Failure to have control over the institutions of society such as the state, industry and commerce is to lose ones independence to the things one has created for his own use. It is ones power and influence over the national economic, political and educational systems that gives dignity the autonomy and freedom to enjoy life. Even a villager likes to feel that without him there is no nation.

Dignity has a central place in the structure of national identity. Dignity alone has the power to influence national institutions to remain faithful to the nation and its people. A nation without dignity relies on the state for survival and forgets that the state is an instrument of the people who create it to protect them.

Finally, even though our dignity is derived from the social reality in Kenya it has broader application in the world especially in the Third World. Americans and Europeans cannot appreciate the meaning of dignity as we have experienced it unless it has some monetary and material value. One notices this when westerners start addressing their cars the same way they address their children or wives, calling them names like persons. The dignity of things as experienced in the western world may not therefore help us to face hardships and transcend the otherwise hopeless situations. It is our African dignity that gives us a common identity as fellow sufferers and which binds us to work together for common destiny. If human dignity loses its influence in national affairs we shall have hollow peace, love and unity.

The prevailing value system in Kenya based on the conviction that commercialism and profit considerations form the basis upon which everything else derives its worth negates all that dignity has influenced us to become. There is more in life than money and power. There is religion, love, trust, cultural heritage and hope which people need besides riches in property and fame.

CHAPTER 3
HUMAN DIGNITY:
THE ROOT OF NATIONAL
CONSCIOUSNESS

When a young woman and man become conscious of their own identities as independent, competent and mature human beings they demonstrate this by building their own home. In the same way a man and a woman leave their father and mother and unite to form a new family, Africans have left their own old tribal identities to form a new national identity. Africans are now sure that their national identity can provide them with the same security, service and dignity as their tribal systems used to provide them. Our national patriotism consists of this consciousness. One becomes patriotic by putting his life, service, energy and loyalty to the nation to justify one's expectation of security, protection, service and acceptance in that nation. Any one who has not invested his life and work in the nation should not expect that nation to recognize his dignity, unless he is a child, mad or deformed. The nation is like a bank into which we put our precious life, service and future, expecting to receive these from it when we are in need or problems.

Our national consciousness has roots in the same dignity as had produced our ancestors' tribal identities. Historical changes made necessary by colonial intervention, scientific and technological modernization and population explosion forced tribes and clans to yield their former identifies to national identity. Allegiance to the new identity and service to it begets a new patriotic spirit of co-operation, love, unity and peace amongst all Kenyans. Our present degree of national consciousness gives national politics psychological acceptance amongst the people of all tribal backgrounds.

We must not forget that the same African dignity that produced tribal institutions produces our modern institutions. Just as our Kikuyu, Kamba, Luo or Turkana

51

traditions had laws and customs by which the tribes were maintained in orderly and secure conditions, our nation has adopted the constitution and legal system by which the nation preserves itself. In the old tribal system of tribal institutions everybody was conscious of his role, functions and responsibility in the preservation of the tribal unity, peace and justice. Institutions were not left to themselves to do as they wished, but were accountable to human dignity.

One cannot be conscious of belonging to the nation and at the same time fail to be affected by the corruption and vanity of others belonging to the same country. A priest serving his country in religious institutions is as guilty of what happens wrong in medical, political, educational, business and industrial institutions as those working in them because all these institutions are one system. While no other institution exerts as much influence on others as the political institution, thus, the state, it would be lack of maturity and morality for anyone to think that he has no responsibility in what happens in other institutions, outside his own. If businessmen were to package their food in bags that were made of toxic material priests, teachers and politicians would be affected by eating that food. The state should not be the only institution scrutinizing other institutions. Environmental agents have a role to play in scrutizinng the way others use water, forests and air. Consciousness is a sense of national identity, not institutional identity. To be conscious only of being a priest in the church, doctor in the hospital or driver in a *matatu* is not only false consciousness, but unconsciousness as far as dignity is concerned. A *matatu* driver should be conscious that his passengers are not goods but nurses, students and guards going to serve the nation in different capacities.

Without a national consciousness rooted in human dignity and manifested in national identity, people serving different institutions and organizations can undermine each other and destroy the nation. I have read of a political state which got tired of the religious institutions of its time, banned them and organized its own religious institution in which the emperor was to be worshipped as god. Indeed, the state is the only institutions that serves human dignity by taxing, registering, scrutinizing, locating and aiding all other national institutions, but cannot become their substitute. It has power to ban, stifle, curb or destroy them if they violate human dignity, but not to act as if it is the only national institution. In Kenya, the state consists of the Civil Administration with the president as its head, the Parliament and the Judiciary. The state must be conscious of its unlimited power and serving them as parts of the same national system. Without a consciousness that the state is at the centre of networks of national institutions, cultural, economic, religious, health, educational and recreational it can be tempted to become everything.

We renounced our tribal institutions and adopted modern ones because they lacked a common modern state to regulate and hormonize them. Rather than the old multiplicity of chiefs with conflicting clan customs, we now have one national system consisting of civil service, courts, legislature and various ministries. This truly represents human dignity. Dignity tells us that, unlike the old exclusive tribal and clan consciousness which we now call unconsciousness, the modern national consciousness embraces all tribes, races and human differences. This brings progress to our nation and enriches our dignity. This means that it is our consciousness that gives rise to the national institutions but not that those institutions give birth to our consciousness. If the national institutions were to be the ones that produce consciousness, the colonial institutions would not have originated our struggle for freedom. The colonial system which was based on selfish British interests would not have given birth to the fight for independence based on African human consciousness. Not one expected that a western missionary would have come to Kenya to teach people how to have national identity in the situation where the mission itself reflected a foreign identity. The aim of foreign missionaries was to destroy our tribal identity and in its place, put a slave mentality.

When Kenyan people identify themselves as Kenyans they feel greater dignity than if they were identified as princes, doctors, teachers, princes or generals of a heavenly kingdom without earthly substance. *Theirs is the majesty, glory, honour and dignity of Kenya.* The distinction of Kenyans from Nigerians, Chinese, Russians or Germans is not in race, colour, religion, class or ideology but in national consciousness. Even a Palestinian refugee struggling to regain his nation, feels better addressed as Palestinian than by his personal name. I care more for the good name of my country than my own personal reputation. The holy and sacred name of Kenya is sealed with the blood of those who gave their lives for it, just as Jesus Christ had given his life to save what he had created, for his example, we must give our lives to the nation which we created in the likeness of our dignity. The realization of our dignity can no longer be an imaginary, fictious or metaphysical task but something revealed in our social conditions.

The constitution of a society represents in the material conditions the truth that dignity contains in the heart, soul and mind of man. The state, under those conditions becomes an instrument or tool of man for helping him to bring into being the values that would dissipate inside man if they lack chance to come into fruition. Freedom, justice, love and other elements of human dignity that would become useless and worthless if imprisoned in the heart of man, find in the creation of social freedom, political, justice and communal love their practical and historical practice.

The practice of human dignity brings into consciousness religious, economic, educational and cultural interests for which the state is a unifying factor. In some cases the dignity of the people brings into consciousness many institutions operating as agents of a central government. The core institution in any given country which possesses a monopoly of power and has absolute and final authority is known as the state. The power and authority of the state may be at any given moment in the hands of the presidency, chiefdom, kingship, monarchy, party, military junta, family, or bureaucracy, which may have acquired it by means of national elections conquest, revolt, coup d'etat, cessation, settlement, heredity or chance. But whoever and whatsoever has the power of the state enjoys a monopoly of force over the territory under his jurisdiction.

Nevertheless, force alone, without an ethic consistent with it is not an adequate basis of a political state. Force without the moral values of human dignity, such as peace, mercy, patience and tolerance is a naked form of violence. Force, when embodied in political power clothes violence with police action to apprehend criminals and keep peace, and with military cover to defend the country. Otherwise a state that lives by use of force loses the loyalty and free obedience of the people and becomes illegitimate. A national state that uses violence against the people who created and sustain it plants the seeds of its own dissolution. The meaning of "possessing a monopoly of force" in the state must always balance with the loyalty and support the state enjoys from the people. You cannot keep force without keeping loyalty, keep authority without keeping obedience. A ruler who continues using force to win loyalty and obedience reduces his people into slaves. prisoners and objects whose will to regain dignity he no longer can control. This is where our people had to fight colonialism, to re-instate their dignity in social institutions, especially in the state.

There is no amount of force in the world that can conquer, enslave and destroy human dignity for ever. Darkness cannot overcome the light. The rule of just law by democratic means is the only adequate political form of modern society capable of rational expression of human dignity. No political or economic organization however justly or morally constituted can bring into fruition the inner dignity of the population which owns it without enlisting their participation and love. On my wedding day, soon after leaving the church compound, my newly wedded wife asked me about what travelling arrangements I had made for family members to attend pictures in the studio and join us in the evening party. I shouted her down in front of our colleagues, and said "shut up. That is not your business". My reaction was based on the fear that unless I subdue and subject her under my newly acquired authority as her "head" she will never recognize my manhood. My new authority and power turned into instruments of violence, coarcion, humiliation and degradation. Instead of trying to enlist her loyalty and obedience through love I used colonial · methods of suppression and conquest. Instead of receiving loyalty and obedience, I received resistance, disdain and dissidence. I was the state, but an insecure state. Despite forcing my wife to recognize me as the state in the new nation, "the family", I was like a "head" without a body.

Thanks to this lesson I had to learn from my mistakes, I realized that unless I recognize, respect and esteem the dignity of my wife, no amount of force shall make her recognize my manhood. Her interests in me, security, protection, order and procreation were not enough to make her forfeit her dignity.

Similarly our interest in the state, security, orderly development, economic progress, social services, and institutional discipline are not enough to make us forget our dignity. It is from our human dignity that the state derives its right of existence and ceases to be our state when it violates our human dignity. The awareness of this moral relationship between people as creators and the state as their creature is what we call national consciousness. People are the ever present but not always visible power of the state like God is the ever-present and invisible power of the universe. While the state created body, people created the state to defend their nation and serve them. They belong to the nation, not to the state. Without national consciousness we lose direct connection with the state and start looking at it as a pre-existent god, always there with or without us. Loss of national consciousness means that the legal systems by which we are governed belong to the courts, police and jailers and not to us. It means that we are uncertain of our lives, our freedoms and our rights because these are in the hands of alien forces beyond our comprehension. A state, not aware of its accountability to the people, like that of Emperor Bokasa and General Idi Amin in the 1970s is a dangerous thing for a nation to have.

Even though all people appear to have some elements of dignity when acting as individuals, tribes, clans, castes, races, classes or other forms of parochial and factional organizations, the central function of dignity is the formation of a single national system with the state as the most powerful central organization from which other organizations derive their security. In Kenya, religious, business, industrial, military, educational, administrative, party, transport and press institutions should be scrutinized to find out whether they have a consciousness loyal to their national state. *Ideological training in Harambee and Nyayo phylosophy should be given to all civil servants with a view to making them conscious of themselves as instruments of human dignity.* A nation without a cadre of devoted and dedicated servants of national dignity cannot prevent the adulteration of the state by foreign ideologies such as Americanisation, forcism and Zionism. However, human dignity does not survive as a philosophy of avoiding contact with foreign ideologies, but as an autonomous practical power of state, slavery, punishment, arrest, imprisonment, torture and even death. Dignity is unbelievably powerful when it comes to its ability to resist arbitrary force and cruelty of injustice. Our people of Africa. never surrendered their dignity to colonial states. They appeared to have surrendered it because they have to avoid being annihilated in the hope that their day of freedom shall come. Had they lost the hope of freedom completely they would have committed suicide by fighting to the last person. The fact that they surrendered their tribal identity to form national identity does not mean that they identified themselves with the colonial state.

In the same token, most of our African government do not serve their people out of the fear of being overthrown, or losing the next elections but because they have long term interests of serving the people. Their interests in their human creators, not their own temporary interests, are their motive behind their social programmes. They differ from colonial governments whose interests was to oppress and exploit the people. In brief, national consciousness is the function of two basic activities in which people create national institutions and in which they have to keep those institutions accountable to the purpose for which they were created.

The way our bodily organs function to satisfy our needs and solve our problems is the way state institutions and their agents should function to satisfy our national identity. Being conscious of this basic relationship between us and social institutions, especially the government is a necessity of life.

There is no healthy and good education if it does not bring children to the realization and possession of this in their consciousness.

Unfortunately, African theological ethics have not paid adequate attention to human dignity as having a central place in measuring whether certain institutions should exist in the country or not. Our national constitution assumes that human dignity remains the same and equal in all people whether they are in power or not. The life of a person does not increase in value when he becomes president and does not decrease at the end of his term of service. If national dignity did not exist in leaders before they became leaders people would not have elected them. The chief end of the state is therefore to represent the aspirations of nation so that through its machinery people can serve one another effectively and efficiently. In the national state people seek the example of national consciousness which they should have in their villages. And since the state does not have enough workers to carry out this sentimental work of uniting the people to feel as one nation, the church, school and other social organizations assume a very important function of integration in the country. All nationally organized institutions have no other moral function except with and for the creation of national consciousness based on the dignity of the people. This consciousness must be logical and practical in terms of the services people expect and receive from their national institutions. If the human dignity of Kenyans were not powerful enough colonialism would have continued until today. Dignity is all that is good for the national institution by which the nation negated all that is evil. Despite this being the case the whole subject of dignity has been left to isolated philosophers, novelists, theologians, politicians and sophists. Fictional writings such as those of Ngugi wa Thiong'o have at times exposed the lack of dignity in the post-colonial economic set up blaming this on the corrupt officials and political decadence. Some novelists deal with lack of dignity in the leadership and glorify it in the poor peasant actors. They blame the root of inequalities to the perpetration of western Christianity and civilization in our society in the service of

58

multinational exploiters. The Kenya philosophy of love, peace and unity is one way the state tries to make people conscious of themselves as the ones on whose behalf the government maintains peace.

For this reason some Kenyan novelists devote most of their writings on raising the self-consciousness of the people toward the harm capitalistic tendencies in the state may cause to their moral self. These cultural writers see politics as the vehicle of expressing and defending the dignity of the people and express disappointment that political leaders are themselves corrupted by economic lusts. Some novelists have become so puritanical and extreme in their attack against capitalistic materialism that they have alienated themselves from the state completely.

The other champions of national consciousness are the journalists, preachers, parents and teachers, the latter three categories being the subject of discussion at a later chapter. The journalists use their power of the press to denounce the celebrities, leaders and organizations that act contrary to morality and justice. Unfortunately the press does not usually discuss morality as a basic requirement of national consciousness until a well-known public figure like a clergyman, politician, policeman, doctor and lawyer is caught red-handed stealing things from his office, smuggling coffee or committing adultery. When a male teacher befriends a pupil and makes her pregnant, government officials misappropriate the funds allocated for the salaries of their junior workers, the doctor steals furniture from a government hospital, nurses carry in their pockets spoons, sugar and salt from the side tables of their patients, a bishop is exposed as the father of his maid's baby, the newspapers and magazines write headlines of such sensational immorality to incite public outcry. This does not go beyond dealing only with symptoms of social decadence, leaving the disease of bad conscious to take its cause. This work of the mass media suppliments that of the church in denouncing social evil.

It might be possible for the press to conceive of dignity as moral principles which leaders must follow out of fear without conscience. I know of pastors who act good to avoid being disciplined by the church. This lack of conscience comes as a result of many years of intimidation by church hierarchy. Exposing an individual to public ridicule and damaging his name may deter others from continuing with evil actions but in the final analysis replaces their conscience with fear. One wonders how national values such as integrity, punctuality, fidelity, and love can exist in the mass media if they do not already exist in schools, churches, courts, hospitals, business, industries and other institutions. The press itself does not grow from heaven and journalists do not have the dignity of angels. They belong where the teachers, lawyers, pastors, police, civil servants, clerks, matatu drivers, armed forces, hotel workers, and street cleaners belong. There is no such thing as corrupt civil servants without a corrupt community to support their corruption. It is impossible to have a thief elected into parliament unless there were enough thieves in his constituency to elect him. The press should therefore look at the social community which votes into power a "sugar-daddy", a robber or liar before assassinating the character of the man the community votes into power. To write sensitional news and cartoons about a minister who steals land from the poor helps neither the minister nor the poor if the community replaces him with another thief. The role of the mass media as part and parcel of the national system is to strengthen human dignity at the community level out of where leaders are obtained. In fact, dignity is not a moralistic individualistic feeling to which the press appeals for commercial reasons but the community power or judging right and wrong and acting upon it.

During the time of local and national elections, the community acts responsibly and directly. But once the community has made the mistakes of electing bad people to run its national and local affairs, it must suffer the consequences of its mistakes by waiting for the next elections. This is for the sake of continuity of law and order. But as long as the community is represented in the decisions and actions of the state, the state has infallable tenure of authority in national affairs.

There is no justification whatsoever to overthrow any state institution unless it suspends the constitution by which human dignity is defended and becomes the enemy of the people like a foreign invader. The great European Psychologist Sigmund Freud argued that the greatest man's drive is sexual self-consciousness, but I say that *the greatest man's self-consciousness is the security of ones human dignity.* In defence of this dignity people in Hungary were known to fight Russian military tanks with fists and Kenyan freedom fighters were known to fight British Empire with stakes. The absolute authority of the state is absolute because the dignity of the people who give the state its power is absolute non-negotiable, inalienable and without other value to compare with. Since people place their trust in the state to defend their nation, the nation being the collective and corporate dignity of all who identify with it, all other national institutions must place their confidence in the state. This gives the state infallable authority in getting rid of corruption, lawlessness and evil in all other institutions, churches, mosques, press, companies, clubs and schools, because all institutions serve national interests.

While the state should not interfere with domestic affairs, how churches, families or charitable organizations are run, it cannot allow these to violate human dignity. If a priest embezzles church money, whatever else the church does to discipline him, the police should arrest those who failed to report the crime to the state. It is demanded by human dignity that there is uniform law for all people and institutions in the country so that justice is done and seen to be done.

Human conscience is not a subjective matter, but adherence to universal moral principles upon which our institutions are founded. Government and other institutions do not have another conscience of their own apart from the one based on natural consciousness and rooted in human dignity. If the state and other institutions persist to be evil people should question their own dignity and national identity and see what is going wrong in their hearts.

Human dignity consists of the consciousness that life is more precious than anything human beings have made, organized, constituted or created, whether culture, nation or government. It is the essence of life that a person retains in himself despite its external expression and manifestations in the social institutions and behaviour. It is being conscious of oneself as greater and more valuable than the man-made state and other organisations that gives man courage to criticize them when they act contrary to his dignity. The Apostles of Jesus Christ died resiting the state laws that required people to worship the emperor who was at that time the state.

National development means institutions that can reflect and promote the dignity of the people. Moral development is essential to human consciousness in order to have moral men capable of building moral institutions. A developed person is the one conscious not so much about the accumulation of money, fame and other trappings of power, but of his purpose and reason of being in this world. Our reason for being in Kenya, as Kenyans, extends beyond our birth and our death. This is the reason we are very deliberate in our instruction of our children because we shall one day die and leave them to pass on the future generations the dignity we ourselves received from our ancestors. *We are not doing a favour to our children when we educate them but are pleading with them to carry on with our dignity.* Children are the extension and continuation of our dignity not our possessions. Inheritance of property is incidental to the procreation of dignity. It is due to the rotten concept of education as a factory for producing "future leaders" that we have leaders who cannot stand for justice and freedom, leaders who can sell their people for foreign grants and investments. They see the essence of life in material economic growth than in the dignity of the people. The human purpose of education is not and should never be to train future leaders but to form in the minds of our chidren a strong sense of self-respect, self-esteem and self-confidence so that they can work with us to continue with life when time comes for us to leave this world. In this process of forming dignity in our children we may find some of these with gifts of leadership, art, science, technology, farming, sweeping, laundry, shoe-making, maize-roasting, cattle-herding, tea-harvest and preaching. In schools children learn how to get along with others nicely and act collectively. The school puts the kingdom of God in the hearts and minds of children so that when they become adults they can be servants of God's kingdom by being servants of their country. To say that the school produces future leaders is not only evil and immoral but a violation of human dignity. It is human dignity as observed and recognised by the population that surrounds a particular personality that produces a leader. The community, not the school, but sometimes using the school as one of the experience, determines what character and qualities in a personality that represent those of the whole community.

The community produces the leader through the vigorous process of testing everybody to find out who leads the others. People dislike living under the bondage of leaders imposed upon them by heredity, education, profession and wealth and whose consciousness is different from their own. *Leadership has roots in the common dignity of all members of the community not in the classroom.*

The philosophy of leadership, and of the school as the institution that produces leadership, was based on fixed ideas that the Kenyan economic, political, religious and social institutions were too archaic to produce leaders without the help of colonial teachers. The school was to function like a factory for producing spare parts so that when community breaks down occurs, a nut misses or moving parts got worn out, brain-washed elites can be plugged in. This was the philosophy of Africanization whereby Africans were being trained as spare parts to put in the place of the Europeans and Asians who wished to vacate their positions after independence. This is where we have hundreds of thousands of spare parts high school and primary school graduates who cannot fit anywhere. The school may therefore perpetuate the conditions that inhibit the growth of the characteristics of dignity required for self-reliance. This is why *the state should institute national service at the end of all academic and professional training.*

If the Kenyan system of education exists to produce the future rulers we should have another system that produces those they shall rule. The present system appears more successful in producing a greater class of unemployed than of leaders. The leaders' fear of class warfare between themselves and unemployed, poor and powerless calls for human dignity as the principle measurement of national education. The leaders' guilt conscience, that they enjoy the privileges that are not available to all, forces them to act arbitrarily toward the under-privileged. They preach the morality of obedience and loyalty to the system because they are in the leadership but not because they believe in obedience and loyalty to the universal principals of dignity such as justice, love, peace and respect to life. If they themselves were loyal and obedient to the people their actions would speak louder than words.

How do you create national consciousness in national leaders rooted in human dignity so that their good work can glorify their Father in Heaven? One way to do it is to make leaders aware that they must command respect from the people without necessarily having to impress them with guns, education and medals. An officer carrying a machine gun and a lady carrying vegetables should in the eyes of the public, represent positive values, such as security and health.

No matter under what circumstances people are living they want to be assured that the soldier carries the gun to protect them and the lady carries food to feed them, and not gun to scare them or food to poison them. This mutual respect and confidence between those in leadership positions and those without specific social positions is the manifestation of human dignity. Recently a woman started delivering a baby in an elevator and all the women around her run away to escape responsibility. Perhaps they felt ashamed of this as an insult to their common dignity as women. But one man remained and helped her deliver the person who perhaps will lead and save the children of those who run away from their problems. The problem of the women who escaped responsibility was lack of ability to lead themselves to things their school education and professional training had not prepared them to do. Our ancestors who never went to school would not have fled away from a birth event. This is the result of western education of "Mind your own business" or non-interference. Yet dignity is an assurance that everybody is a good Samaritan starting with ourselves. Perhaps the spirit of individualism comes from the missionary religion which taught that we dissociate ourselves from this world so that we can obtain rewards in heaven.

National consciousness is impossible under the spirit of individualism that tempted Adam and Eve to think that they must have everything to themselves. They listened to the snake which told them that "you shall be like God" if you take over even what belongs to someone else. We still have people whose main reason for being Christians is to have everything here on earth and in heaven. Rather than their salvation making them conscious of others' interests they think of how they can exploit their fellowmen so that they can bribe God by contributing something toward helping them. They think that by helping their victims of exploitation God will bless them and appoint them to become governors of earthly and heavenly institutions. They like wounding people so that they can be seen providing ambulance and bandages. Harambee projects like clinics, village polytechnics and churches are the most effective tools of charity by those whose pleasure is to make profits by underpaying others and overpricing their commodities. For them, charity is a means of pacifying the victims of exploitation.

Man was created in God's image and continues to receive dignity from God. This distinct act of God's creation takes human form when man breathes life into others through charitable actions without alterior motives.

Aid given to man by man should be from dignity to dignity. Charity is supposed to help people live with one another as children of God unlike the way exploiters use it to help their victims accommodate to exploitation. In the United States of America the victims of social injustice and economic exploitation are given "State Welfare" to help the assimilate dehumanization and indiginity. I used to work for this kind of system in the city of Philadelphia, in 1968, and found the welfare system as a means of keeping alive human beings like animals, without the will and power to free themselves from their exploiters. From my experience of life in the American ghetto as an urban institution marked by poverty and crime, I learned something about the results of capitalism. The most powerful government in the world creates ghettos as a place of run-down housing where the exploited and oppressed members of society can be damped by social forces to show contrast between the nature of sinful man-in contrast to the divine nature of God. God gave man the garden of Eden, a sheltered, protected and prosperous place of pure delight. God loved to come and walk with man in the garden. But in American man creates his own heaven by exploiting those for whom he creates the ghetto where he does not care to come and walk with slum dwellers. In contrast to the God of salvation, the deliverer and Friend of His people, the white man in America refuses to derive example from God, and sets his own example of creating a slum world as an expression of his evil lordship. The whole of the third world is becoming an extension of Philadelphia and New York Ghetto.

Nevertheless, the crucial truths of our history must be sold to all citizens, their children and their children's children, so that the independence for which their forebearers fought and regained may have eternal significance in their lives. Either the independence their ancestors regained is theirs or it is not. If it is their independence, then the question of whether they are educated, trained or employable does not arise. What arises is a more fundamental question of equality and availability of the means of existence. To deny a thirsty man a cup of water is not to recognize his dignity.

In my official responsibilities of Lay Training, between 1976 and 1981, I taught and lectured to people of almost all classess, ages, groups, races, tribes, professions, religions and cultural backgrounds. I baptized both the infants and aged. I talked with both the managers of morturies and the midwives in maternity house. I made friends with judges and criminals, and pitied the prison warders who had to stay awake while prisoners enjoyed their sleep. As a matter of interest, at the Lang'ata area of Nairobi one can observe prisoners looking after sheep, goats and cattle in the fields, relaxed and at leisure, while the prison guards look worried and agitated, making one wonder who would be answerable to the government, the guards or the prisoners if these animals were to get lost. Anyway, I travelled by matatus and witnessed the drivers bribing the police at one stop and being charged with the same offence for which they had bribed at the next stop. At one place my vehicle was caught without reflectors, and after several hours of insisting that I be charged with the offence the policemen agreed. This was my *way of enforcing the police to enforce the law*. I observed in other areas harambee projects abandoned, especially at and around Ngwataniro High School in Nakuru District because the people who had initiated them lost their parliamentary positions. All this experience taught me that the realization of dignity in public life and personalities is not adequately institutionalized, legalized and popularized to form a common conscious and moral conduct for all.

Even in the homes of the people I visited, I found parents as morally confused as the rest of the public. I saw some teachers, acting as parents taking their own children to other schools different from the ones where they taught. One father had to take his children to a school about ten kilometres away from the neighbourhood school where he himself used to teach and for the same classes that he was teaching. Instead of working hard to improve the standard of his school, he worked hard to buy a car and transport his children away to where the standards were better. It is surprising to find civil servants, including police officers, employing watchmen and keeping fierce dogs to protect their families from harassment by night burglars. How do these law enforcement agents expect people to feel secure if they themselves are not secure in their homes in the very neigbourhood where they are employed to keep security? There is no point working to provide a service with which you yourself are disatisfied, as in the case of working as a doctor, in a state hospital where you cannot allow your family to be attended in case you expose your loved ones to more problems. We should follow human dignity, thus, treating others the same way we expect them to treat us, as the common moral criterion upon which to minister to the needs of others in community, including our own.

We should stop regarding success or failure as the moral measurements of human dignity otherwise the ethic of the "end justifies the means" will continue to prevail. According to the criteria of success as upward economic mobility, even

67

thieves, robbers and murderers tend to win the crowns of honour and glory once they "make it". *The church itself finds attracted to thieves who have achieved success and aligns itself with them.* It is most likely that the church will regard as God's blessings the stolen property of rich men who after success want to help the poor.

The Organization of African Unity is part of this success morality when it blesses coup d'etats that succeed to overthrow the government and condemns abortive ones. Our history, in the most regretable manner forgets its righteous and ordains as saints its notorious lunatics. This is because our national consciousness has allowed itself to be falsefied with the foreign ideas of success as right.

In my study of human dignity, which was apart of lay training programmes, I found professionals, especially civil servants, administrators, teachers, nurses, magistrates and doctors are the most difficult category of human beings to extract a healthy national consciousness. They are so used to being employees of the national system that it has become difficult for them to see the nation as something greater than an "Uncle Thom", from whom to extract a salary. They are so neurotic about their jobs, homes, bicycles, clothes, hair-styles, furniture and official cars that they do not see the moral value of the state as being different from a cow from which to milk money. For them dignity depends on the position or rank one occupies in the *hierarchical bureaucracy,* so that those working in the provincial offices feel superior to those working in the district offices. If anybody possesses something which appears more expensive than of another, whether clothes, shoes or house, he becomes the object of intense envy and might be harassed to abandon his job by those of higher ranks. This is because material wealth is associated with the position one occupies in the bureaucracy, thus making it very difficult for juniors to enjoy their jobs when seniors do worse than them economically. But *dignity prohibits anyone to demand more from the society or government than he has invested in it* by his service.

This brings us to the question of how our religious institutions can allow this kind of bureaucratic mentality to possess the keys of heaven while it lacks the keys to open its closed mind, now being locked behind materialism. Religion should function to arouse and strengthen human dignity by relating to human action and institutions and by removing contradictions between dignity and action. So, our main concern in this discussion on dignity and human consciousness is not that we have no good institutions in our society but that at times there is a conflict between what we are, our dignity and what we have created, our social institution. How to remove this conflict is our main objective in teaching, preaching, serving and work. When human dignity is excluded from our works and organisations our community becomes irrational, governed by blind economic mechanisms in which all progress is but a temporary mixture of opposites.

My desire for a strong state is made on the ground that it is a state based on national dignity in which the good of all has replaced the antagonistic structures of a materialistic and individualistic anarchy based on self-interests. This view of the state is different from that which argues that the state is immune to and above love, respect, justice and other things that constitute dignity. Advocates of this divorce between state and dignity argue that the state is there like a murderer who after repenting cannot restore the life of the man he killed. The state is composed of those who enjoy wealth and power after gaining them through corruption, deception and intrigue and who cannot recompense their victim whom they must rule. If we were to ask the state to have dignity it would have to lose its power and authority in its attempt to achieve reconciliation with those forces it subdued in order to gain power. Arguments like these are nonsensical in that the men who made them confess not only Christ as their Saviour but to have dignity. How can such people have a government which they pray for, call their own, and at the same time deny their ability to shape, form, old and create it in accordance with their own nature? The same motivation that makes us to pray before choosing a marriage partner, house to live in, and food to eat should motivate us to pray for a just state.

No possible cure can our society find for obsession with

one's own salvation as attainable only in his heart and mind, and not anywhere else otuside man. Relucant to grow up, or afraid of doing so, people want love within the heart without expresing it by means of political, economic and social institutions. This lack of maturity makes people dependent on the devil for their social and political decisions and on Christ for their spiritual and personal decisions. There was a time when some of our Revival Brethren refused to vote during national elections as a way of protesting against the behaviour of the local members of parliament. It was corrupt for them to measure the dignity of their country by the immoral behaviour of certain parliamentarians, who fortunately lost their re-election, because such measurement presupposes that any state is inherently immoral, which is not true. *Dirty politics exists only in the attitude of people whose minds are dirty.* One people without dignity to share with others fear to expose themselves politically.

It also means that we have holier than thou members of our society who due to self-righteousness would prefer dictatorship to being involved in democratic responsibilities. From Uganda we have learnt that evil men can succeed into power quicker and more easily than good men, and that soldiers can obtain with bullets greater power to do what they want than civilians with ballots. The easier it is for men to get access to political power the easier it is for them to get access to other people's wives, money, privacy and lives. Hence, better makes the mistake of voting into power a politician who turns out to be corrupt than wait for a dictator to impose himself. In fact, better a corrupt state within our power to change than a corrupt one outside our power to do anything. My conviction, with Hegel, Pains, Locke, Mill, Marcuse, Socrates, Plato, Calvin, Martin Luther, Saint-Simon and other European whom I have read share with me, is that the state is a product of human reason and civilisation, like other products such as religion, art and philosophy and that like them, it is there to satisfy human interests, not man to satisfy its interests. On one hand it may be his father, as Plato thought about it, but a father born by human mind. For this reason religion should never be used as an excuse not to participate in state affairs because this would introduce antagonism in the mind which produces both religion and state leading the insanity and destruction of the personality that carries such antagonisms in himself.

One cannot remain human in his dignity if he confines his life to his inner world of what goes on in his mind, soul and body, without concern about what effects the outer world of his social environment has on his inner one. The inner world of dignity and the outer one of work, interests, products and institutions must be correlated and homonised in the creation of a national state consistent with human dignity.

Children learn the effects of what goes on inside their parents and teachers not by only listening to them but also by observing their actions. They do not therefore emulate their behaviour from books, sermons and pictures alone but also from the behaviour of their government when dealing with tax payers, its employees and prisoners. Unlike adults who believe that children learn by gaining size, weight and information, children learn by gaining dignity. The development of this dignity may be retarded by the cruel behaviour of the adults in the environment, but nevertheless children can distinguish what is wrong or right by the fact that nobody enjoys being hurt. The dignity of heroes who died fighting for freedom, such as Dedan Kimathi attracts children more than that of their parents who impressing them with huge houses, big cars, and exclusively expensive suits. Children prefer to see dignity in dead heroes who suffered for their nation than in successful criminals who enrich themselves by sucking the blood of innocent and powerless workers.

And why do the righteous lack courage to fight for the control of the material and human resources by which social structures are maintained? In the situation where power is in the hands of armed forces or politicians why do the righteous refrain from being armed or from capturing a political seat? The fear of the righeous to become involved in wordly affairs turns their righteousness into "criminal" negligence. We remember the freedom fighters because they were almost sure that the colonial forces would kill them if they joined the struggle for independence, yet they put their dignity before self-interests. Jesus Christ himself became involved in worldly

71

affairs and accepted to die on the cross in order to restore dignity to humanity. Then, why should those committed to money appear to work harder for the attainment of their goals than those committed to dignity?

There is a great deal of dignity to learn from Hosea and Micah who prophesied against official corruption during the height of economic and political development in Israel. The two prophets considered mercy and justice toward the common person as integral aspects of national dignity. Lack of mercy and justice, they prophesied, would bring tragic consquences to the whole kingdom and its rulers. *Mercy meant doing justice to the poor not because they were poor, but because, they too required their needs to be met* in order to enjoy life like others whom God creatd in his own image. Even rich people needed help if something unjust caused them not to enjoy being the children of God. Any king or priest who as a result of spiritual bankruptcy neglected to include the poor in his personal or national budget sinned by acting in an indignified manner toward those he caused indignity. The whole Old Testament regards it as incomplete consciousness any human consciousness not aware of the existence of the government in its prayer, thinking and activities. When God punishes the state for its sins there is nobody who does not suffer, even the innocent. Our concern for food, housing and security shows how much we must be conscious of the forces that have control over national resources. In search of dignity human beings are conciously uprooting themselves and breaking away from not only their traditional systems of power but also from their colonial habits of dependence. It is in this struggle for dignity and against the forces that oppress and exploit them, both modern and traditional forces, that people safeguard their self-respect, self-confidence and freedom. In this struggle they believe that national leaders are with them if not against them. Without human dignity national leadership is nothing but worthless, with greedy self-indulgence, selfishness and evil intentions. This is why we should be conscious of our national leaders and pray for them before every meal, in private and public.

On the whole, lack of dignity in civic institutions and personalities does not necessarily lead to lack of allegiance to public institutions and officials. However, this allegiance may be based on the fear of the civil war, social instability and disorder rather than on love. In order for social institution and public servants to maintain dignity they must represent and reflect the aspirations of the people and be able to gain satisfaction in the role of being representatives whether they are paid or not. Their own national commitment and never their salaries is what would give national identification its moral authority. The problem is that even without the danger of ever missing their monthly salaries in a developing and poor country, there are still soldiers organising mutinies, doctors and teachers going on strike and others moving from public service to private sectors for pecuniary reasons. They forget that they live in a society where economic inequality, unemployment and poverty are still the dominant threat to national integration.

Finally we have certain individuals in society who know how to assert themselves in artificial and special ways. They may be lawyers or teachers, politicians, wealthy and land and real estate owners with many tenants, brokers, consultants with a lot of clerks and secretaries, chairmen of clubs and local associations, party officials or just men of overwhelmingly strong personalities. These individuals can ruin society if allowed to practice their influence in contradiction with national morality. We should device ways of controlling, containing and regulating their socio-economic and socio-political conduct. If their decisive moral element is to win votes, sell their goods at unreasonable prices, get bribes from clerks wanting promotion in bank or manipulate people to vote in certain ways, the result will be the corruption of the whole society, the victory of the baser instincts in political and social life. Some shopkeepers and builders belong to this class of individuals who lacking strong commitment to the creation of national identity do exercise moral mediocrity in character and intellect. It is hoped that those who occupy such artificial roles of influence in society can work together with pastors, civil servants and others in public institutions to force a national morality based on national as argued in this chapter.

The future of our society depends on the extent to which we can promote national consciousness based on human dignity at all levels of national leadership. This cannot be achieved without a coherent view of human dignity and the encouragement of voluntary action among religions to help the government maintain moral standards. The desire for moral consciousness politicized and directed to the attainment of national goals in what we have been discussing as national consciousness. Consciousness for self which is not consciousness for others with whom one forms the nation is psychological death.

In the next chapter we shall discuss how dignity is gained and passed on from one generation to another.

CHAPTER 4
HOW TO COMMUNICATE AND RETAIN HUMAN DIGNITY

4.1 THE ROLE OF PARENTS AND OTHER PILLARS OF DIGNITY

This far, we have found human dignity to be the behaviour appropriate for harmonious existence in a given social and physical environment, the nation.

You may, by now, have wondered how and when this dignity is communicated from one person to another, from generation to generation and what are the proofs that the agents of transmitting dignity are in possession of dignity. Dignity is communicated through varieties of social relationships the commonest of which are of parents to children, teachers to pupils, preachers to congregations and institutions to members. Like a pot rests on three stones to have the food in it cooked, a child rests on the home, church and school to have society form dignity in his personality.

The manifold processes of passing dignity from one generation to another start when a baby is born and his needs force him to co-operate with the physical and social conditions. Such environmental conditions leave the child with no other choice but go get along with nomadic, urban or agricultural life. If born in a Manyatta the child immediately adjusts to the smells and voices of sheep, goats and calves before he gets used to his father, and if born at Pumwani Maternity Hospital gets used to the noises of jets that land at Easleigh Air Base. The whole national system of life, politics, religion, economics, press, music, sports and architecture gets introduced to him by the behaviour of nurses and parents long before he can distinguish them from one another. Some parents may require that their child get circumcized and his ears pierced on the day of birth to mark his gender, clan or nationality. The child's experience, smells, tastes, sights, what he hears and what touches him, crystallize into the behaviour that conforms to his environment. The whole life of a person from birth to death is spent on how to control the environment and ones relationship with it.

As children continue to adopt and adjust themselves to their physical and social environment they acquire the techniques, skills and values that make them benefit from their environment. They conform themselves to what they enjoy and struggle against what threatens their lives. As they grow and become adults they refuse to inherit the models of existence that perpetuate their toil and misery and perpetuate only those forms of life that make life worth living. They start defending the institutions that give them satisfaction and reject those that deprive them happiness. This consciousness of what is good or bad starts to create the moral and economic basis of dignity. Unlike other animals which reproduce their behaviour by genetic codes, instincts, human beings reproduce their behaviour by a life-long process of educating children in which the family and the school becomes the social means of behavioural self-reproduction. After school, education continues through ritual, ceremonies and socialization until the grave. This eternal process of learning is what increases human dignity. It is our ability to organize and manage ourselves in relation to the world that gives us the meaning and purpose of living, that is, human dignity.

Societies have found that socialization by use of select cultural values, objects and institutions to integrate people into their national society is more consistent with human dignity than the use of coerce, conquer, colonize, enslave, torture, imprison or threaten them to conform. Dignity produces voluntary behaviour in which people relate to each other by observing certain traditional, legal, customary, affectionate or acceptable standards, below which they might hurt one another. How to ensure that our children shall relate to one another by the just, legal and contractual standards that we have set, and will not start enslaving and hurting one another when they take over the management of national economic and political behaviour from us is the greatest task of education.

Human beings are mortal beings. They immortalize themselves by succession. Before our children can inherit our wealth, power and national institutions they are therefore taught to behave like ourselves so that they can continue with development from- where we have stopped. Whether they revolt against our methods of survival or not, we must train them what food to eat when hungry, medicine to take when sick, clothes to wear when cold and games to play when lonely. They may want to punish and condemn us for having had given them *"githeri"* and *"ugali"* rather than *"spargetti"* and *"cookies"* but experience will teach them that we did not give them sand and ashes to eat. The fact that whatever they eat will help them to inherit our dignity will be more significant than whether they have changed from eating "boiled potatoes" to eating "potato chips", have ceased using "spears" to using "bombs". Proper parenthood is the ability to sustain ones offspring to the point at which it can sustain itself. The present generation of which the school is a parent and the church a home by extension, does everything within its capacity to condition the next generation to carry on the work of procreation. This procreation is more than a hereditory process of one generation giving birth to another; it is a process in which we make sure that others, coming after us, carry in their bosoms the same likeness of God as we have inherited from our ancestors. The more we are involved in the creation of a future society the more we feel the pain and shame of whatever in our society harms the just, loving and peaceful likeness of God in us. If the well being of our children is ours, then we shall not communicate to them warlike values that appear like giving them sand and stones to eat.

Disharmony and dichotomy in the behaviour of the present generation communicates the basis of future social conflict and political disorder. The most important functions of communicating dignity are therefore the selection of what behaviour to transmit, how to organize that select behaviour into a curriculum, and creating an environment, both at school and at home, which children must have in their behaviour. Education for dignity, therefore assumes direction, control and guidance of children to acquire dispositions that make them partners and sharers in the habits that make our society just and sustainable. All our children, the poor, lame, deaf, blind, crippled, orphans; of all races and colours, of all classes and ethnic backgrounds receive education together in the same school which functions like an extended family or simulated nation.

To educate our children in sharply marked-off classes of schools would distort and corrupt the behaviour of our children by adding to our ethnic differences class ones. The school is national and social, not racial and class. This is because a school cannot reproduce and perpetuate factional or group behaviour without creating in the character of its graduates antisocial and inhuman attitude toward others belonging to other factions and classes. In order for education to produce behaviour appropriate for harmonious relationship in society the methods and means of communication must be standardized, rational, universal and co-ordinated between the parents and the state and by the state through society's representatives.

Having common behaviour to which everyone subscribes his loyalty and obedience does not therefore come automatically without deliberate and organized methods of choosing the material for teaching and paying the teachers. Less expenditure in the upbringing and training of young people and more expenditure on the construction of police stations, courts, prisons and guards to cope with increased defects in human behaviour shows lack of dignity in the school curriculum.

We should not therefore think of bearing children for whom we have not the will and resources to become their models of mature culture and identity. The community should discourage from becoming parents, teachers and pastors those immature adults who lack resources, time, will and proper values to communicate to their children. Proper values are those desires, believes, preferences, perceptions, needs, dispositions, opinions, goals and aspirations that are conducive to orderly social existence and contribute to the well being of the whole society. The ability and capacity to have children should not therefore be determined by biological maturity but social maturity in which the parents can provide an autonomous, self reliant, free, pious and peaceful habitation for their offspring.

While all adults play a parental role in society, none is as close and intimate to the process of the social growth and development of dignity as the parents. The press, hospital, business, theatre, army, sports club, church, political meeting, and court may be the best places for children to go and observe the behaviour of adults and see for themselves how dignity operates but children can be easily confused by all this if their parents are poor models of national dignity. In the family, the parent mediates the security, health, justice, order, knowledge, affection and peace that the national society, through the state, mediates in terms of law and order. When the child enjoys justice and respect on the family he extends this joy to others in community and this becomes the foundation of his future behaviour as a manager of industries, a president of a country or a sportsman. Some social institutions like beer halls and gambling casinos are the results of having families in which children lacked proper religious and moral guidance to resist falling into temptations.

People do not therefore support national institutions because they are forced to be loyal, devout and dedicated to them but because they help them to practise what they learnt during childhood. The heads of our schools, companies, hospitals, armies, parties, churches and firms become new fathers and mothers away from homes and parents. The dignity of obedience to our parents that we formed at childhood becomes the dignity of obedience to our president of the country during adulthood. The state, is then the only single institution that fulfills and completes our dignity because it takes over from where our parents left in the work of suppressing sinful, bad, wrong and injurious behaviour and encouraging peace, love and unity. The family and the state therefore must work hand in hand to produce dignity in children, from kindergarten to university, leaving to the state the work of continuing with the discipline of adults. The family may have a role in disciplining the adults through moral, social and religious sanctions, by public opinion, but the major task of seeing that adults do not commit crime, dissidence, riots, corruption and laziness belongs to the father of the nation. the state.

4.2 WHERE DIGNITY BEGINS

Every human being is at conception carrying the potentialities of dignity. But it takes about five to seven years to form the intellectual foundation upon which the mind of human being can form independent and own behaviour, distinct and unique from that of those who produce him. A child is supposed to have a mind of his own when he can rely on himself to avoid wrong, bad, harmful and sinful behaviour and to pursue behaviour appropriate for him to survive in his environment. In Kenya, we have perhaps unconsciously, accepted six years of age as the standard age in which a child can act independently without the assistance of parents and can go to school to be taught by the state what will be proper behaviour in the nation. The state, or government, at this age joins the parents and helps them for about sixteen years to build upon the six year foundation a life-time foundation. While a child is born with latent mental faculties for developing and appropriating dignity, a brain potentially and perpetually capable of forming behaviour, he is not born with any behaviour worth dignity.

Indeed, except for his physiological body, the child is the opposite of adult behaviour, dependent, irresponsible, demanding, yelling, crying and egocentric. To free him from himself, to rehabilitate his uncontrollable movements and prevent him from self-destruction, that becomes the hardest job, even harder than feeding, clothing and sheltering him. A child is born with the behaviour that all the adults do not want and therefore join hands to tame it. The goodness about this chaotic, disorderly and irrational behaviour is that it is innocent, as innocent as clay in the potter's hands. The disciples of Christ were offended by this innocent behaviour but Christ welcomed it and likened it to the kingdom of heaven. Why? Because you can form out of children's behaviour any behaviour you want. A child is a young mini nation which if properly founded will have peace with itself and others.

When a child is born, the doctor helps the mother to give birth to baby, but the mother and the father help the child to give birth to his own dignity. For a child, dignity is simply the behaviour approved by his parents, right behaviour.

Parents help the child to form respectable behaviour by directing his desires, demands and actions to particular socially acceptable ways of getting his needs satisfied and by blocking those desires, demands and dispositions which would be harmful to either the child or others if pursued. The earlier the parents help the child to get along with others the quicker the child learns to cope with the social and physical environment. When our first-born started supporting herself with chairs and tables, she tried to reach the flowers wishing to tear them off and put them in her mouth. A certain grandparent saw me become very annoyed with my daughter and trying to look for a higher table where to put flowers beyond her reach. He got amused with how my daughter was causing me to behave in a funny and irrational way and said, "Leave the flowers where they are, let your daughter try to reach them, then say 'no' to her behaviour and pinch the fingers with which she touches the flowers". I did exactly that, and to my amazement, my daughter never wished to bother the flowers again. She also learned the meaning of the word "no", and from that one "stop", "sorry", "please" and "thank you".

A child is therefore not born with dignity, he is born with the faculties of capacity and ability to form dignity. The needs that drive a child to adjust his behaviour to what pleases his parents are like the survival instincts that compel a dog to learn the will of its master and avoid displeasing him. The difference between a dog and a child is that the dog continues to depend on right stimuli for right responses and never forms the behaviour in which the stimuli and the responses become integrated into one action. My daughter did not only stop breaking the flowers after reforming her attitude toward flowers but made sure that flowers were taken care of, watered and placed in the right place. Human behaviour is a synthesis of all reactions to social and physical conditions to form an acceptable mechanism of how to react whenever similar conditions recur.

For survival reasons, children do their best to conform their

81

behaviour to that of adults. They also go beyond conformity by repeating, modifying and transforming the behaviour they have learned from adults to see whether it can operate in new and different situations. You may have observed children organizing dolls and toys into families where two of them act like parents telling others to behave properly. They try to reproduce the behaviour of parents and other adults in themselves and to modify it to suit their situation. When a mother talks with her baby, with good gramatical language, day after day, for many months, the brain of the child picks this as a stimulus that affects it to form a mental structure of her mother tongue. The dog in the house may hear the same sounds the human mother makes to her child but lacks the mental ability to code, respond and repeat the behaviour expected in response to the sounds. The structure of language which we call "mother tongue" becomes formed in the brain of a child long before the child is capable of logical, organized or intellectual response and interpretation of what it is forming. The cumulative experiences of a child, whether in language, play, weather changes, affection or hunger help the child to form personality traits or ways of reacting to external stimuli we call behaviour mind. When many external stimuli demand the child to respond, and especially where these stimuli may require conflicting reactions the mechanism of selecting to what to react to first and in what manner is called attitude. The mind is therefore the behaviour shaped and maintained in the brain by the experiences and consequences of previous interactions by the child and its environments. All states of mind, feelings, traits of character, instincts, attitudes, manners, likes or dislikes, fears or courage, security or insecurity, hostile or hospitable, friendly or aggressive, and so forth, are products of the original experience of a child in its interaction with others in the environment and cannot be easily rubbed off in adulthood. Habits is second to nature. There is not a single language capable of describing human behaviour. Some of it requires moods, drama, isolation, war, archeology, philosophy or music to communicate but cannot be exhaustably communicated. Learning starts when one is born and stops when one dies. Gramatic endowment of the brain, besides the environment, is the most important factor in the formation of human behaviour. The effect of environment upon the child cannot produce better personality than the brain of a child can handle or help to produce. Princes and princesses may grow up in the best social environment the kingdom can afford and receive the best education in the empire but acquire less capacity and ability to survive and function properly in their society than others growing up in poorer social conditions. Personality is the capacity and ability to maintain ones dignity under test. If one can survive deprivation, criticism, opposition, loss, or pain without losing faith in himself or without getting upset and collapsing, he has a better personality than the one whose moods change according to changes in the environment. This capacity to acquire national, logical and organized approach to changes in the environment depends on the genetic facilities with which one is born. Even such complicated behaviour as religion, warfare, engineering, law, architecture, phychology, morality, city planning, mathematics, chemistry, physics, strategies, biology, electronics, aeronautics, sociology, some of which occurs in thought, requires natural gifts in the brain that those without them cannot have it. Not everybody has innate brain equipments of learning abstract complex behaviour, like theories on dialectic materialism, or St. Paul's doctrine of salvation by grace. But everybody can be coached by others who are more intelligent than him, and after much drilling acquire good Christian behaviour according to Pauline theology. Language communication is the most complex human behaviour. Over 90% of Kenya system of education is done through the medium of language.

Kenya schools are aware of the intellectual differences in children. They keep on examining children to know how much time to spend teaching a child and how much effect to expect. Examinations should not be there for lowering or raising the dignity of a child but to enhance dignity by teaching a child what his brain is capable of handling. Any child denied opportunities for education is denied his realization of dignity which is a basic human right.

All human beings are born with desire to learn, learning being the ability to remember previous experience so that one does not have to suffer again when faced with similar problems like the ones which he suffered in the past. We all behave according to the pressures and demands of our social physical environment, to avoid repetation of painful encounters and relive pleasurable ones. We form behaviour according to our success or failure to avoid, cope with, manage, escape, alter, adopt, utilize or deal with issues affecting our lives. If we cannot overcome them. Otherwise we surrender to difficult issues like famine, poverty and diseases and become their slaves. Some behaviour is acted in thought, for instance, meditation, trust, faith, peace, joy, love and mercy and issues in actions like ritual, dance, prayer, eating or friendship. But all behaviour whether occurring only in mind or issuing in external activities portrays the nature and value of the person behaving. The child pursues these things which to think and do provoke others to notice him as worthy their love and praise.

You may have noticed that children avoid being ridiculed, laughed at, mimicked, scolded, discredited, abused, insulted, blamed, ignored and shouted at, and like being praised, given attention, loved, praised, touched, listened to, credited, admired and rewarded. As a Sunday School teacher I avoided what children avoided and liked what they liked until they came to see me as a better parent and teacher than they found at home or school. One child wanted to take me to his home and show me where he had hidden his waste matter, in the closet, to punish his parents who had beaten him for having had lost their panga in the grass outside. When I taught the class how bad it was to do something without permission from parents and how the Prodigal Son was forgiven by his parents after repentance, the boy revealed his problem with his parents to me. At his home I discovered that the parents never gave their son any chance to confess his mistakes but only scolded, rebuked, reprimanded, punished and alienated him. He had to retaliate by causing them to feel bad smell in the house. Having done many contacts with prisoners and ex-prisoners, I now know people who become rapists, burglars, robbers, thieves, arsonists and vandalists, just for the sake of retaliating against the society which they imagined was denying them jobs, promotion or education. Such people may have been products of upbringing in families and schools where parents and teachers gave them negative treatment. Adulthood has good or bad roots in childhood. Bad adults are products of bad childhood. Behaviour is a long road of experience and consequences from home to school and from school to national and international forums, assemblies and organizations, a road which one may die at seventy years having travelled only a small fraction. Some people are born, raised and live for a century without ever getting mature. They die babies of many decades having children and grandchildren, but without mature behaviour fit to be self-reliant in their own environment. They lived their whole span of life in their cradle where the village, family, custom and nature made it easy for them to survive. They became biologically adults but not intellectually and morally. It is this kind of immature adult, without complete development of their innate abilities and whose mental gifts are underutilized who when given responsible positions fail to cope with society, its morality, law, justice and love and have to be given new cradles in prisons where the prison walls and guards can provide them with substitute homes and parents. The work of prison warders is to give them parent guidance, thus, rehabilitation and skills, that they missed at home and school during their childhood. There is a Swahili adage which says *"Asiyefunzwa na mama yake anafunzwa na dunia"* which means "He who is not taught by the mother is taught by the world".

Once people become adults before their behaviour matures you cannot help them by caning and scolding because that is what they consider as arbitrary authority. Immature adults are still children who to retaliate against society have to use bombs, teargas, rockets or whips to terrorize those who they matter in the closet to use smell as a tool of exerting his own infertile counter-authority we have a lot of men in authority who cannot see face to face with offenders and rush to use violence to communicate their lack of dignity. International wars are caused by the infantile behaviour of leaders who want to hit back at the world because it denied them proper love and affection during childhood. Dignity begins at childhood and matures as one grows old.

4.3 SUBJECTIVE AND OBJECTIVE COMMUNICATION
Dignity is therefore communicated by a community of parents, teachers, pastors and other agents of society to children through the power of example, influence and organized institutions. The society associates dignity with all institutions whether any specific individuals possessions, occupying or representing those institutions has dignity or not. When parents misbehave in front of their children or national leaders turn into dictators families and nations do not set out to abolish them but to punish the individuals holding these offices at specific moments. People are expected to have dignity first by virtue of being human and secondly by virtue of their status or role in society. The dignity once gained through childhood, youth and adulthood must be ploughed back to society through service.

The missionary zeal to convert all African children to the objective behaviour found in Europe without any regard to the role these children were expected to play in their social conditions in Africa was very harmful. You cannot convert people to have moral, ethical, legal, religious, political or economic behaviour in their minds without at the same time expecting them to change their environment to fit what is in their mind. Similarly you cannot change the environment without changing people's mind and expect peace from them. All civilisations are the result of people trying to change minds to fit environments or environments to fit minds and so on. Any behaviour of a person which does not issue in practical activities to change environment or the environment that people cannot comprehend and change to accommodate them cause suffering to the whole society. When the missionaries taught African children the behaviour appropriate for Europe they without intention trained them to become nationalists in order to make that behaviour appropriate for Africa.

Therefore, communication becomes a form of changing behaviour so that it becomes less threatened by environment and can use environment for its own advantage. The goodness of any behaviour is in its ability to control environment at a minimum cost to its chances of survival. If it costs your life to manage your environment to your own advantage your dignity loses meaning and its value becomes less than what it tries to gain. You only sacrifise your life when you know that there are possibilities of others benefiting at your expense.

We therefore contribute the greatest dignity to people who can sacrifise their lives for others as our fore fathers did by fighting for independence. Jesus Christ also died for our benefit. In other words, one is most dignified when acting on his own, freely without compulson, and without fear of being punished, killed or laughed at for the benefit of his country. The aim of education is to communicate that this is the ultimate aim in child development.

Self-respect is the subjective aspect of dignity which requires winning respect from others in order to attain satisfaction. Self-respect is the subjective side of the same coin of which others recognize that you are worthy respect. If you respect yourself and fail to win respect from others, your self-respect is a kind of insanity in which you imagine you are what you are not. If you have self-respect it must come as a result of your interaction with others in the social environment in which others appreciate you as a good father, mother, teacher, policeman or doctor. To be not respected by others reflects lack of self-respect. Those who will become future parents and teachers must grow knowing how to respect adults especially those who occupy positions of social responsibility. The same case applies to self-confidence as a doctor whether the patient who comes to you dies or as a teacher whether the child in your class passes his examinations. Self-confidence remains only subjective without objective reality if it is the mere feeling of oneself as good for something which others may not recognize.

To communicate self-respect and self-confidence to children requires a lot of models for their behaviour until such time as they can continue with the behaviour on their own accord. Once children attain respect and confidence in themselves as capable of behaving like their parents and teachers on their own, without fear of external pressure, then they must be left free to exercise dignity on their own. The measurements of what one is worth is to have self-respect and self-confidence when left alone to act freely. To attain such maturity of dignity, one must have gained self-control and self-direction in the many competitions the home, school and church had provided for him.

This is why sports competition and academic examination are important to dignity, because they strength self-confidence. If the society elects someone who has not gained self-confidence, and self-respect to a leadership position, as a managing director or bishop he will feel insecure and start attacking all those under him he thinks were more qualified for the election than him. Churches, companies and governments expeience a lot of turmoil, bickering and bureaucratic upheavils when people without self-confidence are appointed to lead those with self-confidence. We know a lot of church and school heads who need more motherly care and schooling to gain self-confidence than they need to make tough decision. The only tough thinking such immature adults can do is how to persecute their opponents. The more examinations one had experienced in young life, whether he passed or failed them, the more self-confident he became to handle his environment. When a person fails to mature in his dignity and remains an infant in his self-assessment he finds it difficult to laugh with those laughing and finds it hard to cry with those crying. A person is immature when for his dignity he relies on his parents or teachers to feel self-confident and in the absence of teachers after reaching adulthood, relies on external stimuli for his behaviour. A mature person should be able to recall from his previous life experiences certain attitudes and considerations that he requires in order to deal with a new situation. By the time one is eighteen years old he should have been exposed to enough surprising situations that nothing in his future life comes as a real surprise.

From birth to six years therefore a child must acquire the formal structure of mind by which to acquire skills of helping him to exist in his culture, and from seven years to adulthood build upon that structure of mind the habits worthy self-respect and self-confidence that would last him throughout his life. Such habits must be cultural and correspondent to those others in society will respect and admire. They must be good social and cultural habits. Culture is these habits of mind which in practical reality others appreciate. We normally think of culture as ways of life, how people treat each other, how they raise their children, how they cultivate their gardens and keep their animals, how they organize and govern themselves, and the ends to which they devote themselves. I therefore take culture to be habits of avoiding to die sooner than nature allows and making life comfortable and enjoyable. Culture is all that one has learned from his society as behaviour proven by trial and error, and through scientific development as the most suitable for existing in a given society. I do not expect a man of eighteen to twenty five years receive better cultural and social modification of his behaviour than he has already received in earlier years. Society must therefore prevent conditions from allowing children to reach adulthood before it puts in their experience aspects of cultural behaviour such as religion, architecture, government, art, science, history, technology, agriculture, music, veterinary, military, business, linguistics, medicine, aeronautics, astronomy, ballistics, mechanics, administration, cooking, driving, nursing, picking coffee, packaging or sweeping, depending on the mental capacity of learners to benefit.

Culture is therefore the objective reality of human behaviour of which human habits are the subjective. A culture which no longer shapes human habits is merely an acheological, library or museum material.

The natural habitat of culture is human behaviour, thus, how ordinary people live, their religions, dietary, political, economic and social habits. There are times when cultural values may not be the cure of personal and social illness and be the chief means to mental illness, reducing thinking to nothing more than trivialities and moral "cliches". There are times when my culture does not make sense to me. The religious culture in Kenya is full of quacks from America, evangelists of sexism and spiritualism from universities, swams of slum dwellers, poor and oppressed, all in the name of cultural development.

My grandparents had dignity concentrated in their personalities so much that I felt dignified touching them, listening to them or even thinking about them. Nothing in the present world, not all the studies, prayers, friendships, promises and social progress, can give me so much dignity as being named after the name of my grandfather. The God who created the universe and communicated himself from generation to generation through all my ancestors down to me must be the same as God the Father, Son and Holy Spirit or else the very idea of God is nothing but nonsense. It is this cultural orientation that molded my childhood into self-confidence.

Without relating the name of God to the God of my grandparents, God who for millions of years has preserved the genes and hormones by which I am alive, you would be telling me of another god inferior to God the Creator and Sustainer whom my grandparents worshipped under the trees facing Mount Kenya. I was indocrinated and trained by every woman of my grandparents age that I am her husband because my grandfather married one of them, my own grandmother. This was vicarious marriage in which the one man and the one woman repeated what our Adam and Eve, Gikuyu and Mumbi had done, by submitting themselves to God to carry on creation by procreation. My whole community inculcated me with the dignity of being an argent of creations most supreme value, that is, continuity itself. When I got married and started to have children I felt happy that I have not disappointed my grandparents, and through them, God. My grandparents had received their dignity from their community by means of traditional culture, ritual, custom and religion. Their culture was simple, homogeneous, coherent and easy to communicate through bodily behaviour, language, artcrafts, customs, myths, beliefs, attitudes, habits, ways of doing things, music things, music rituals, plays, drama, instruments, tools, ornaments and other objects. My grandfather passed this culture to me while looking after our cows, sheep and goats by means of oral instructions and visual demonstrations. This he did more effectively than my parents who taught me Christianity and western values by means of books without adequate cultural demonstration.

The culture which I am transmitting to my children is more complicated and complex than the one I live myself because it lacks harmony and unity in any specific generation and personalities. It is a culture of alienating objects unrelated to one another, consisting of telephones, photographs, video tapes, computers, T.V. transistor, movies and telex and other lifeless impliments. This material culture has not become natural in Kenya the way my grandparents models of communication had become to my tribe. The present culture is full of windspread failures in agriculture, mass media, population explosion, economic crimes, political corruption, social disorder and moral decadence. It makes dignity sick of materialism, pornography and anxiety. This is why we need more psychiatric clinics in Kenya.

We may not want to limit the communication of dignity to subjective values and methods, that is, subjective experience and perceived reality, but it would be hurtful to human dignity to think that only those with radios, papers, telephones, books and T.V.s can have dignity. Oral, personal, and human interaction in its most natural and emotional sense still remains the most effective mode of communicating dignity and supersedes all other means and methods. Objective means of communication, whether in logic, theory, abstractions, science, philosophy and mathematics and whether through material objectives like cassettes, video, radio and papers would not satisfy human behaviour and its need for love, attachment, love and play as the family and home communication does. Parents should therefore spend more time with their children in order to influence them with cultural dignity.

4.4 DIGNITY AS BIRTH TO GRAVE SELF-DISCIPLINE

Dignity is not only the best you can to realize your potential energies and make human benefit of your behaviour, but also attaining satisfaction with what one does with his potential. Thus it is the discipline one gains as he meanders from birth to grave taking each moment in life as a gift from God that sustains dignity.

There is no dignity without restrictions at all. Every society has its own "ten commandments". In Kenya we limit sex to marriage, wine to ceremonies and death to accidents and natural causes. Despite that thousands of people die every year, people get addicted with wine, and sex is practised out of marriage. The society does not arrange schools for training people to have to excel in such conduct. Nobody discusses with his friends how to kill himself or his with enemies how they can kill him. We confine talking to certain limits. On the other hand we allow people to fight or kill in self-defence if attacked by others planning to kill them. Even a man condemned to death is not allowed to desire death and kill himself. Arrangements are made by authorities to execute him and prevent him from executing himself before the appointed time. Discipline is the measurement of acceptable behaviour in any given circumstance in a given society. Customs, morals, traditions, beliefs and theories are all social measurements of acceptable behaviour in any given circumstance in a given society. Customs, morals, traditions, beliefs and theories are all social measurements of acceptable behaviour beyond which there is no reward. This discipline may mean avoiding death by eliminating whatever is intending to cause death; eliminating our enemies or befriending them. Befriending the source of trouble is better than causing more trouble to it, thus, arresting a killer before he kills is better than killing him. This is why Jesus Christ died to reconcile the world and the United Nations has instituted machineries of dialogue and disarmament. Discipline is best when it is self-discipline, thus, initiative to win and befriend, rather than responding to other's bad behaviour by our bad behaviour. Reconciliation is the art of befriending the enemy in order to preserve his life.

While living things may be easily crushed by others stronger than them they nonetheless tame them and use their energies to further their own existence. Self-discipline is the ability to preserve oneself by preserving others, receiving honour from those whom one has honoured, gaining respect from those one respects and planning no evil. It is the ability to make your employees believe that they work for themselves, not your company, pupils know that learning is for themselves and not for teachers and parents and that peace is for warriors and not only for their victims. So, self-discipline starts when we gain behaviour appropriate for living with others without hurting them or allowing them to hurt us.

However, it is easier to discipline others by conquering, coercing, subjective, enslaving, colonizing, impoverishing, imprisoning or even torturing them, than to have discipline in ourselves. Stopping others from harming us is easier and cheaper than stopping ourselves from harming them because; all we need is to run away, escape, hide, fence or exile ourselves. This behaviour of seek and hide in what is called law of the jungle where weak run away from the strong and start chasing those weaker than them.

Since sex and money are the most common sources of irregular behaviour we need to know how people with an African cultural background can accept western behaviour without getting sexually and pecuniary hurt. In the African society sex existed in mutual and friendly relationship in which pleasure and procreation were the main motives.

In America, which is typical of western civilization, sex is always in the mind of businessmen, clergy, journalist and teachers because of their inadequate socialization about it. Before a western women gets involved with "another man", sex on her mind had happened a hundred times with other men, long before the fact. The western man is like a sexual tempest of desires which explode before they reach any specific target. He is a bundle of psychological troubles that make him aggressive to other men whom he sees as competitors. International wars appear to be outlets to many sexual troubles in the minds of many western leaders. They want to prove that they are men, not human.

The fondest hopes of a western man are achievements, successes, victories, glories and other demons that rush out like rockets ready to reach their female target and destroy her. Whatever dominates a western man, if it is not sex, it is money. Money is lifeless and dead and therefore the easiest thing to manipulate. If it is not sex or money which dominates, it is alcohol. This unholy trinity of wine, money and sex is in such great disharmony that the mental agony it produces in the psychology of western society spills over to Africa. The western man becomes to masturbate his pressures by making profits where African becomes a female partner, the object of exploitation. In the western culture sex is a masculine battle against women, a conflict in which man kills the woman morally and spiritually by using her as a means to an end. Signs of indiscipline are so many that chaos appear like the order of the day, it appears like discipline. Such false discipline means perpetual conflict in which to win battles and not people becomes the aim; commanding fear and not loyalty becomes the goal. One seeks sexual pleasure and not fellowship, power and not authority and quantity not quality. The cunning are more than the wise, warriors more famous than peace makers. Western culture sells the vital things of disciplined life like "loving" a woman to indisciplined one like "having" a woman. Having things like sex women, wine, money, positions, titles and status becomes more important than being human. Being is replaced by having. You end up having celebrities who possess feminity or masculinity, boasting of money and sex as their loot and booty, and with very superficial consciences. We do not have dichotomies in our African culture. A person should have a strong conscious-ness of himself as worth living without having to fulfil any condition imposed upon him by his desires for foreign cultural values.

Our society communicates not sexuality or materialism but communicates self-discipline in which sex and possessions are mere expressions of inner self-confidence and self-respect. There is no attempt to exploit others to satisfy oneself because satisfaction is not sought in having but in being. When a child is born he learns from parents and teachers that he can gain pleasure and gratification by giving the same to others.

4.5 HOW TO HARNESS EXPLOSIVE ENERGIES INTO DISCIPLINE

Definitely a child is born without discipline at all. At his birth he starts to see the world as his and his alone. As time goes on he becomes egocentric, acquisitive, tyrant, terrorist and greedy, using his parents as means of satisfaction. He becomes a bandle of every selfishness, as self-assertive, as a Russian or American president. He wants to test his nagging outcry like chiefs of staff test their explosive weapons. By the time a child is one year old he would not give peace to anybody, at night or day until he is fed, his nappies changed and locked to sleep. This kind of chaos, allowed only to generals and colonels after *coup d'etat*, and enjoyed only by heads of super powers, demonstrates the potentials a child has of being an intelligent and productive member of society. A good parent sees such a chaotic and limitless behaviour as a mighty Zambezi river-fall awaiting engineers to harness and make it useful. The parents and teachers become the first engineers of a child's behaviour to harness it and make it disciplined. Every energy in a child is latent material for forming human dignity.

The child of two years enjoys such unlimited freedom that unless carefully watched nothing short of self-destruction and death will restrain him from getting what he wants. He will jump into the river, fire and pit latrine to see what is there. He is completely adventurous, full of ideas and desires that nobody in the world can satisfy without making him sleep. To make a human being out of a child of one to two years is the most difficult task because it means dismantling a king from his kingdom. The aim of parenthood, and of education is therefore to reorganize, direct and discipline a child, to disarm him and win him to become human. This transformation, while very intensive at childhood lasts throughout life in a very extensive manner, in law and order.

The child is disciplined by having his heart or soul reduced to the size of others in society, having his ego measured by that of his parents and neigbours. He has to learn eating when others eat and stopping helping himself everywhere in the house. He is forced by the sheer force of public pressure to stop claiming more times for eating and sleeping than others. He has to queue behind others. A child who used to get a fruit and cried when asked to give it back, such a capitalist, begins to fetch fruits for others. This does not happen until the combined forces of the home, school and church have conquered the wild animal, called the child and subdued it to become human. Yes, it may take four years to stop a child infringing upon the rights of others and intruding in their privacy, and sometimes it may take parents punishing and restraining him physically. Parents in my culture know not only how to take the string out of the freedom of their children but how to do so without destroying their initiatiye, inventiveness and creativity. Soon, children learn to be happy by pleasing their parents and through the parents the rest of society. The less the child depends on parent for his guidance and discipline the greater the dignity which has grown in him. Then a child reaches age six when he can join his parents in the work of teaching dignity by teaching himself. He becomes self-teaching by copying and playing the role of his parents in the family. Children enjoy patterning their behaviour with that of their parents and beyond that with that of nurses, teachers, police, chiefs and others in the society. If any adult is culturally backward, that is, he cannot ride a camel in a nomadic desert society, cannot wash his hands before eating in an urban society, or cannot avoid getting hurt by vehicles in a busy highway he should not be allowed to stay with and guide children's behaviour. Children should not be given toys by adults who cannot distinguish right from wrong, good from bad, and beautiful from ugly, unless there are others to interpret this to them. I have already said that the society is full of adult children who may be children of four years at the age of seventy. Children whose fathers stay away from home and come only to bring money to their wives should have abstained from having children. This is because passing genetic features from father to child is what animals do without passing on any cultural trails to them. Human dignity is not genetically transmitted but culturally communicated through teaching self-discipline to children. Parents are therefore responsible for the behaviour of their children and should never bear any without the resources of making themselves available to them. Such resources one self-respect, indpendence and self-reliance, and the time to be with a child to demonstrate the character of dignity.

There are values of life other than material resources people can communicate to their future generations. Children may hear about the death of their relative when at school and ignore it until they go home to see the reaction of their parents. When an intimate friend of our family died, our children heard about it while at school and did not know how to act until they came home. From school to home their feet were shaking and their mind confused because their feeling had no experience in letting out traumatic disturbances. Once they reached home they noticed our sorrowful behaviour and begun to become sorrowful. From them I learned that sorrow is a cultural behaviour of letting loss and pain burn themselves away. Grief, I learnt, is the deepest and most intense form of sorrow and burns itself out quickly due to its nature of burning intensity. It consumes a lot of mental energies, and within a few hours or days destroys itself peacefully. Weeping, like Jesus wept when he heard that his friend Lazarus had died releaves the mind from anguish so deep that not to weep would explode the mind into insanity.

This is why dignity is a whole life and life-long discipline in which there are ways of crying, weeping, trading, eating, worrying, healing, helping, working, learning, playing, serving and walking, not just doing anything the way one likes.

Those unable to conform to acceptable behaviour must introduce new, alternative and better behaviour as we already know in the way Africans construct their houses differently than they did in the past. For those who cannot conform to acceptable behaviour and have nothing but disruption to offer they must be severely punished and rehabilitated.

However, just as you cannot force your child to grow ten centimetres more overnight, do not force people to learn proper behaviour one day. Learning is a form of growth similar to physical growth, in which what is learned transforms and becomes a part of what is already there.

In addition to behaviour being the total experiences one has undergone in his life it is tendencies toward, against or away other people's behaviour. These tendencies away from, against or toward others are inner-directed and sometimes quite unconscious. A white man may not know that he is a racist in his behaviour against a black man until he becomes conscious of his dependence on his past experiences of domination over others. One must be able to detach himself from traditions and dependence on them to revaluate their significance in the light of new circumstances otherwise he remains a slave to his past conditioning.

Some teachers and parents have erronious views that children become stubborn in order to gain attention. The need for attention is only a symptom of self-assertion when a child wants to be recognized as one in charge of his own behaviour, having already declared himself free and independent from external control. A child knows that if he throws himself in the mud, parents will feel the pain of dirt and mud more than him because they are the ones responsible for washing clothes, but not for his behaviour. Stubborness is a form of vengeance which may lead a teenage to commit suicide to make his parents suffer the pains of being childless. When a child is forced to reach a point of not wanting his parents while his parents still want him he can punish the parents by destroying himself. It is therefore good to make children know that they can have independence without having to fight for it and that they are not possessions. Even husbands can be babies to their wives and refuse to eat or sleep in order to punish the wives who they think need them healthy to earn "bread". However, it is essential part of discipline to administer punishment to children by caning or depriving them some sort of pleasure so long as this does not reinforce stubbornness. An authorized person like a parent or a teacher can strike a child of three years by hand on the "bottoms", of five years by a cane or of ten years by anything which can inflict pain. Children of over ten years can be deprived tickets to attend sports or go to cinema. God gave pain to children as a way of helping them to sense the limits of their behaviour. On the whole every child should be exposed to every form of social discipline while still young. He should learn the business of life from birth to grave. Sex education should not be delayed until children learn how to play sex without moral guidance. In my culture children were taught by their grandparents how sex plays a role in the birth of new babies and why it should be practised within marriage.

The relationship of husband and wife into which most children in Kenya are born and raised is the most effective communicator of sexual discipline. Children observe in their parents the dignity of mutual respect and obligation and identify with them their wishes to have their own married life. In marriage children learn that adults experience security and dignity.

Human sex must therefore be taught as the most intimate expression of love in which the physical body becomes the vehicle of fulfilment. Dignity is in marriage at once individual and corporate, and finds perfection in sharing, especially their sharing feelings, emotions and intellect. This is why sexual relationship should not be confined to emotional and physical contacts and must be expressed in social and religious contacts. Sex outside marriage cannot fulfil the deep desires to secure in the hands of the other and to be guaranteed this security by social and cultural sanctions. Only a longlife union of parents brings mutual love for one another that children born in that union can identify which and emulate for themselves. When the spirits of parents long for one another children observe the mystery of feelings that flow from parents to them. I liked to hear my father and mother arguing an issue because as each tried to get his or her point a cross, and the emotions were high, the debate resolved itself into calmness and tenderness beyond human comprehension.

Parents affection and care of each other as husband and wife becomes not only contagious to children's personalities but gives them good lessons for sex and marriage. Once one marries at age twenty five she has already seen in practise the context in which sexual behaviour has security and dignity. You can observe children below five playing games in which some pretend to be wives and others husbands and sharing "food" made of inedible toy material. This way, children enact the structure of marriage and sex life they see at home and simulate how this shall become when they become grown ups. The society therefore communicates dignity as the birth to grave self-discipline in which people behave according to their interests for survival. Dignity is therefore life management in which the common man, or the ordinary *mwananchi* is allowed to run his life the way he wants so long as he does not interfere with how others run theirs.

Dignity is not manufactured and communicated mechanically by children and youth but is acquired through learning and by choice. Sometimes we are forced to unlearn the behaviour that puts us into difficulties and leads us to sin. To unlearn behaviour is not to undo our knowledge of Swahili, history, mathematics, science or religion but to change our attitude about these where the knowledge does not help us pursue life in other relevant ways. We learn to meet human needs which if they cannot be met by what we know we unlearn it and learn new things. During colonial times we had learned that manual labour is inferior to a clerical job under the employment and supervision of a white man. We would not have learned how to employ ourselves and become job creators until the bitter experience of high unemployment forced us to unlearn previous dependent behaviour.

The reconstruction of experience may therefore communicate dignity by freeing us from habits, formalities, customs and traditions, and at the same time helping to gain by our exposure to them. Experience is the ultimate ground for human dignity and besides being the originator of dignity keeps on renewing itself according to new challenges to life. Experience is as close as we can get to knowing how society communicates dignity in life. Learning experience is the most effective way of acquiring dignity in childhood, adolescence, and adulthood but as we have discovered is what forms the structure of human dignity and mind.

CHAPTER 5
THE DIGNITY OF SELF-RELIANCE, SEX, MORALITY AND LEARNING

5.1 THE GLOBAL CHOICE AND CONTEXT OF DIGNITY

Moral independence, self-reliance and self-discipline prevent human behaviour from operating out of context and beneath human dignity.

In Kenya, we have young and old people who lack good manners and fail to be self-reliant, self-disciplined and sexually moral because the context in which they learned dignity has changed, and the clan is no longer there to give them support.

We have a lot of physically able-bodied high school graduates who after they leave home and school prefer to stay idle, jobless, childish, dull, bored in life, having parasitical mode of existence, because they think the available jobs of milking cows, drying fish, cutting sugarcane and sisal, picking tea and coffee and hoeing shambas are beneath the dignity of learned men. They have a colonial mentality of what an African "English genlemen", must do to earn a living. These false "learned gentlemen", with their false view of dignity without context, lack self-reliance, self-worth, self-trust and independence, end up having trouble with the forces of law and order. They have an infantile mentality that the world, government, church and society are there to wait on them, to spoon-feed and then sing to them a lullaby. We have many views of dignity out of tune with our national context, but no dignity can be dignity out of place.

During the registration of Kenya citizens in 1979, a man was reported to have killed himself in protest that his wife and other women were given identity cards. Before this time only men used to be given identity cards. The card had become, in reality, the identity of that man. To issue identity cards to women, was therefore, to his opinion, tantamount to devaluing and reducing his male identity to a price beneath his masculine dignity. Indeed, this man was like many Kenyans who lack the moral, independent and self-reliant behaviour capable of sustaining itself and accommodating changes. Many white people left Kenya immediately before and after 1963 because they felt that independence was a form of special European dignity which would be spoiled if shared with Africans.

We read in the Roman history that the Roman soldiers preferred to kill themselves, "commit the Roman fool" rather than get captured by their enemies, because captivity would reduce their dignity to nothing. The Jews considered women and gentiles as having less dignity than male Jews and prohibited them from entering the temple. At Corinth men sent Chloes to Paul to complain that the liberation of Christians from the Greek culture, due to the Gospel of Christ, was making women and slaves to reject their subordinate status. Chloes had made sure that Paul understood the plight of husbands and slave owners whose wives and slaves regarded their freedom in Christ as freedom from subjection, servitude, degradation, devaluation and dehumaniza tion.

The new order of freedom in Christ, and the old orders of Romans, Greeks and Jews were at variance with each other. The Romans believed that dignity comes from the sword (atomic bombs). The Greeks believed that dignity comes from civilization, thus, architecture, sports and science. The Jews believed that dignity comes from the law of Moses. But the Gospel of Christ freed all from man-made dignities and preached dignity as the likeness of man with God his Creator Christ was the true likeness of God the Father and only in Christ were people able to have this likeness in them. Other human dignities compared with the dignity of Christ were less than universal dignity and limited by racial, sexual, national and cultural barriers.

I know of people who ruined themselves psychologically and economically trying to maintain in an expensive hospital, a relative who had become unconscious, in a coma, bed-ridden for months beyond medical or surgical hope of recovery, because they thought of it as beneath their dignity letting such a relative die naturally. We shall see whether it adds to human dignity to use money, machines, medine and other modern inventions to maintain a person alive in a negative state of unconscious existence in which a person can no longer communicate or receive communication of any kind. The context of human dignity is natural and social environment.

We accept the unreasonable demands of relatives, especially from parents, who unlike wild animals which hunt their own food, expect us to clothe, feed and support members of extended families, cousins and nephews, who deliberately stay out of jobs to depend on others. The hunger for approval, praise, fame and admiration within our clans, and the fear of bad publicity, makes us lose our independence and act beneath our dignity. Some Kenyans have gone to the extent of dressing bodies of their dead parents with expensive suits and putting them in coffins that cost them a fortune in order to impress members of the public with family dignity. Some nations end up spending more on military hardware to impress viewers during national parade than they spend on books to educate children and fertilizer to grow food crops. They see national dignity as impressing outsiders than as being able to guarantee education and food to every citizen. Dignity is not dignity unless it has a family, community or national context in which it proves its own value.

While we think of practical morality, independence and self-reliance as the most concrete ways of manifesting dignity, we cannot exhaust the list of examples concerning how Kenyans and others in the world elevate themselves above their dignity or lower themselves beneath dignity. Some people think that dignity is spiritual self-reliance. During the Mau Mau period some Christians believed that no imperial or nationalist power had the ultimate authority over their lives. Having given their allegiance to the blood of Christ they were not prepared to sacrifice this for taking any other kind of blood. While not against political independence they were against taking the animal blood that the Mau Mau offered as an oath of allegiance. Theirs was the freedom to die with joy rather than exchange their spiritual independence for political independence. While this was due to lack of proper theological training, it however proved that just as Africans were mature enough to die for political independence they were equally mature to die for spiritual independence. Both parties, the Christians and the Mau Mau believed in independence, spiritual or political, as the ultimate form of dignity and sacrificed their lives for what they believed. Their conflict did not arise out of lack of dignity but in disagreeing with each other what kind of context that dignity should take, heavenly or earthly context.

People without a national identity by which to measure and judge what behaviour constitutes dignity tend to act irrationally and inconsistently. There are cases in which people feel guilty, sorry and ashamed of themselves because of getting poor, losing jobs, failure in examinations, and not getting what they want. Such people associate poverty, joblessness and failure with lack of dignity. In other words, they see no difference between being found poor and being caught stealing. Anything that deprives them attention, appreciation, public notice and fame is considered beneath dignity. But a person may choose to offer himself to be poor to invest his dignity in the service of others as did St. Francis of Assissi. People can endanger their own lives and those of others because they have lost the hope of ever catching up with those with whom they compare their dignity. They feel bitter and resort to alcoholism, crime and anti-social behaviour because their moral consciousness, or lack of it, depends on circumstances. They can feel hostile against those they think denied them positions, jobs, status and power and can organize henchmen and tribesmen to overthrow legitimate authorities. This dependence on social, political or economical conditions for dignity, and reliance on external and alien factors for dignity cannot endure the kind of hardships the nationalists endured in the forests and in detention camps and which prophets endured preaching what they believed. For some people missing comfort is like losing their lives. It is like a fashionable woman who wanted to take away her life because the wind blew off her clothes in front of her admirers.

Let us think of a girl who in the middle of her secretarial training discovered herself pregnant and got herself into conflict with the counsel she was receiving from her parents, teachers, pastors and doctors, who all felt that pre-marital pregnancy was beneath their class dignity. She later discovered her feminine dignity in the context of suffering and in defiance against the adult counsellors who had vain notions of dignity. You can imagine the moral dichotomy of having been brought up to believe that your life is more valuable than anything else in the world and being faced with the question of having to terminate the beginning of life for someone else, just at conception. Not that your parents, teachers and pastors ever commanded you "Thou shalt never abort", but that they were so pleased with your birth that they keep on reminding you about your "happy birthday" during its anniversary. They have taken through kindergarten, primary school, secondary school and are now paying for your college tuition at a national secretarial college to emphasize to you how valuable in dignity is your life in Kenya. You have just discovered that you have a few weeks' pregnancy and now you wonder what would happen to your dignity if you terminate that pregnancy. Your dilemma is what would have happened to your life if they had terminated your life when you were a foetus of one month. Now you are faced with the question of having to preserve the life of your prenatal baby or execute and terminate its life prenatally. You cannot call any story from your grandparents saying that the most greedy hyena ever consumed its young. Neither the family nor the college knows the intensity and depth of your psychological agony, having discovered that the doctor of your college clinic. who made you pregnant is also having his daughter in the same college as you are. Your doctor sugar-daddy is already married. You are torn between the moral dilemma of the conscience your family, church and school formed in your dignity that life, at all stages in its development is worth more than studies. Your studies are just a small selection of whatever else you have learned from your culture to equip you participate meaningful in the national social structure of modernization. This does not take place in a vacuum but in the context of the cultural arena your society has inherited from the dignity of many generations.

You start feeling severe headaches due to the mental conflicts of many unanswered questions of what it entails to become an unwed mother. You ask permission from the head of the college to go and see your parents without disclosing to her the nature of your problems. You feel you have the problems and they have the solutions. You have not learned self-reliance. You decide to see the sugar-daddy doctor who made you pregnant to see what help he can give you before seeing your parents. He offers you money to pay another doctor for your abortion. He tries to convince you that abortion is not murder and that it is alright if done for health reasons to heal your headaches. But the doctor he tells you go go to for the execution of your unborn baby is the family doctor and a great friend of your father. He is one of those "learned gentlemen" who wrongly equate professional success with dignity in spite of lacking moral integrity.

Still in the middle of this moral dilema you think of going to see your local pastor, who occasionally does chaplaincy work at your college, to advise you what to go and say to your parents. He is also your family counsellor and a great friend of your mother. Your mother happens to be the chief of the church woman's guild. You find your pastor, who is also a member of the college board, is facing an equally difficult moral crisis of his own. He is in the process of acquiring a new motor vehicle as a donation from the local politician, your father, who is vying for political office in your local constituency. He feels an irresistable desire to have the car irrespective of having been warned by the church members that political gifts are covert bribery and that it should not start in the House of God.

The pastor discloses to you that he cannot give you any advice for fear that your father might regard it as interference in his domestic affairs. He confesses to you that once this vehicle becomes available he will be able to behave like other members of your college board who take secretarial trainees out for dinners and counselling. You discover that the pastor is as hooked by your father as other members of your college board. Your father, as the chairman of the board takes your headmistress out to parties as often as he takes the trainees out to lodgings. The pastor sees nothing wrong about this modernity as long as there are psychiatrists in the city to deal with the problems of those whose minds cannot cope. He tries to convince you that if psychiatrists cannot help you overcome your guilt and shame, after the abortion, he will ask the bishop to give you a special sacrament to cleanse your conscience. You get more depressed by finding out that the leader of your church cannot survive without a car in the culture where spiritual values have surrendered to material ones. He has forgotten that the rotten fruits of independence come from a tree whose roots were dignity.

You have nobody else to turn to because your teachers, doctors, pastors and peers seem as determined to partake in the culture of modernization and development as your parents who dominate them. You have two things left, to obey your conscience or obey the call to participate in the rotten culture of national progress. You feel that you better commit suicide than disclose to your parents your problem. Everybody tells you that your mother is the Woman's Guild's most wonderful counsellor who takes girls, made pregnant by your father, for abortion, to your family doctor. All her friends talk of unmarried mothers as useless and worthless. You have heard her quite often, say that premarital motherhood is beneath her family dignity. She has, recently, hinted to you to use contraceptives, if you want to play about and still complete your professional training. Like other women in her Christian organizations, she is so obsessed with economic development that her life exists solely to achieve development. She has sacrificed self for wealth. Neither the **Protestantism** nor the Catholicism of her community by which she was brought up can rescue her from her dilemma. You can only swim through your mother's, father's and teacher's culture to a crisis that awakens you to your singular identity and power In the crisis you discover yourself to be an autonomous woman. Then you realize that since your father retired from teaching, started his private business and became rich, he has corrupted everybody in your community and is a member of almost all church, school, and clinic fund-raising committees in your town. He has corrupted the headmistress of your school by donating more money to your college fund than anybody else. He has put in his pocket all the local pastors by helping them to raise money for church building fund and cess. He has enriched your family doctor by sending him all the women he makes pregnant for abortions. To whom do you go to for moral advice, spiritual guidance, motherly care, and rational decision, having turned to your school, your church and your house, all in vain?

You turn yourself for decision only to discover that you are an equal in the nation not a dependent. For you the problem of human dignity has become real and interwoven with religion, politics, law, and money, to the extent where you cannot rely on anybody, parents, teachers or pastors, but on yourself. Your parents, teachers and pastors are no longer interested in being but only in having. What you are is to them nothing compared with what they want you to have, your marketability as a trained secretary. They are all interested in the economic aspects of human relationship in so far as these can bring material benefits. The child in your womb threatens this kind of money market in which professional training is a part. Your people have all become materialistic at heart, for ever seeking after gain for themselves, their churches, homes and schools. They are willing to sacrifice and help you offer for sacrifice your unborn child on this altar of corrupt development. Your father is the archpriest of this god of immoral development which requires worshippers to bribe their victims to keep them silent. Your father himself is the one who provides money to your mother to bribe the school girls who he makes pregnant to keep quite. You therefore wonder what your father, who is the chief sugar-daddy might do if you refuse him to arrange for you instant abortion. You also feel that you cannot have your abortion done in secret because the doctors will have to consult with your father to avoid future trouble. Your question is how best to resolve your crisis without involving anybody and dragging the whole world into it. What you want is the solution not an extra crisis. You want independence and not dependence, equality and not inferiority. You have learnt that your models of successful men and women are in the camp of the devil and you in another dignity. You now turn to yourself for all the assistance you need. You pray to God to help you decide what to do to overthrow the structure of parental, teacher and priestly domination in your mind. Your father is a forceful example of life in the social economic structure of moral corruption in which everybody regards you as the *ipso factor* heir. You are the only child of your parents. To go it your own way is like forfeiting your inheritance. Your parents are typical of the successful individuals in Kenya who due to harvesting the windfalls of the coffee booms, the easy credit, bank loans and Africanization, lost the warmth of human love and care and have become petrified and emotionless in their view of life. For them dignity equals money, sex and power. Success has derailed their values and devalued their dignity to nothing more than being slaves of materialism. You have prayed to God to help you renounce that materialism which to renounce is to say goodbye to the teachers, policemen, pastors, administrators and doctors who worship it. Note you do not know what will happen to you having denounced the worship of your father's god of material achievements. But you now feel that you are the centre of your world, the genesis of your new self, a self-born woman, ready to give birth to your own child. Your behaviour in the world changes the world into your world and makes it different from the world of your parents. This new world streams from your womanhood, from your dignity. You have now added a female perspective from your own dignity to all relationships to which you are connected.

At this decisive moment in your life you lack parents, teachers, pastors, doctors and friends and you feel friendly to the child in your womb. You now feel that you have to produce your friends by bearing them and coverting the world. You need love, not money, dignity, not profession. The very God who gave you dignity at your conception gives dignity to the child of your conception. This is what the girl of your age in teacher training, secretarial college, high school or nursing school experiences. The same happens to girls in universities. Their ethical values are transformed, modified, and decided by themselves singly and lonely, not by the society. What you have in the womb is more than another human being, but a person to love and help form appropriate behaviour for dignity in your society. In fact, the dignity God gives at conception is so unformed, undifferentiated, amorphous and shapless, that like spirit, it has to be forced into forms and shapes by the kind of crisis you have gone through. While others feel threatened by your unborn baby, thinking of him or her as a future **competitor** who will prevent you perpetuating the world of your parents, you start seeing him or her as a future companion in fighting that immoral world. It is a world which spoiled your virginity and now wants you to execute an innocent child who it has to eliminate before coming to share anything in the world. It sees your child as a "time-bomb", a "population explosion". But is only through the crisis of your pregnancy that you discovered your autonomy, independence and uniqueness and you come to appreciate the fullness of your womanhood.

While you must share your dignity, human care and love with the person inside your body, you must also see that you continue with your college training to encourage others avoid having to be misled by sugar-daddies like you. Having resolved your conflict and done it singly, you have a testimony of self-reliance to give to others on how to avoid a crisis of that nature. Whether your classmates want to get pregnant and abort to avoid frustrating their parents desire for progress or to stay virgins, that is their choice. But having experienced the world of money, sex and power, and its hostility to the unborn, its exploitation of women and its heartlessness, you can become their wonderful counsellor. You can help other human being, men and women to draw, write, speak, express and work out their own dignity as well. Your dignity becomes born again in a school of life. You have now become "learned lady", a living text book of historical truth, full of testimony for other young women and men. You now have your own destiny in your hands. Allelluya.

While a child and material progress are not mutually exclusive of each other, and you can have both, your society has not answered the question of when to start and stop having children, at what stage in life. One does whatever affirms her personality, grace and virtue. You have determined for yourself that moral life, with or without material success cannot be inherited, donated or bought, it is the essence of personal identity and dignity. Other women may have no choice to bear children because they bear them to fulfil their biological and cultural prescriptions. But for you, you choose to bear your child in defiance of your parents, teachers and doctors.

Having decided that you cannot abort, you announce to your parents, teachers and others that you can face the consequences of your mistakes, sins and corruption. No bishop, father, mother, teacher or doctor can liberate you from that. Only God can. You feel that you are the one to blame for your sexual play and not the sugar-daddy. You take the full responsibility of your behaviour and believe that nobody else in the world is accountable to your actions. An adult of your age, with the physical maturity of conceiving a child should be culturally competent to rely on herself, not only for decisions of what to do, but of how to deal with the results. Now you learn to take sex seriously as a gift by which you express yourself, who you want to be, and not a permit for others to exploit and abuse your body. Sex becomes an expression of your dignity.

You have learned that sexual intercourse is more than the release of animal drives, it is a relational encounter with the community through another person. Your relationship with the society as expressed through sexual experience with another human being shows you how the society can exploit, neglect and destroy you by its use of a sugar-daddy. The sugar-daddy who abused you and put you into moral difficulties communicated to you the moral decadence of men in high positions. While sex itself ended with the intercourse, it left you beneath your dignity. You have now learned that the true dignity of womanhood, and indeed, of manhood, is obtained through the medium of sincere and responsible relation that culminates in complimentary sex and love. This is impossible between men and women using each other for physical and natural impulses, without mutual love and obligations to each other. Experience has taught you all

111

this. You can now testify to the world that every aspect of our human bodies, including sexual power should be used as an expression of dignity and not as an instrument of exploitation. You therefore, feel sorry for others who sleep with men who have no intention of marrying them who desire their own daughters to be morally behaved. But you remember Zacheous, who after accepting Jesus Christ became conscious of his materialism and asked God for forgiveness. He never went back to his pastors, parents and teachers for counselling because these were educating their children to become like him. Zacheous found his dignity when Jesus set him free from materialism, and from his shame and guilt. You therefore, feel no self-reproach for your past sexual immorality but write a big letter to the sugar-daddy with copies to your parents, teachers, and pastors, pronouncing your forgiveness to him. You forgive him because your image or womanhood is no longer centred on sex, money, development or profession but on the dignity of life itself. Like Mary the mother of Jesus you have a son. So you discover that the sugar-daddy who caused you all this agony is like a Zacheous who needs public exposure and social therapy, and if need be affiliation. This is besides paying your maternity bills. Without dignity you cannot have courage to force men to pay for their mistakes. Your will and determination to prosecute the sugar-daddy cleanses you from this connections, and gives you a new understanding of effective woman-hood as successful motherhood. In this process, you bear a son whose father you have forgiven and forced to pay the cost of his upbring. You can do this without guilt because you see things through the eyes of your dignity and not as an act of sex for material gains. Your new self-realization nullifies the counsel of your pastor who said you needed psychiatric help.

You can now confidently speak to your son, when he grows up, that you did what you did to have him because you used to be immoral, but after having him you repented and reformed your character. You can say to him "When I was a child I spoke like a child; but when I became man (woman) I put my childish things away." To put child things away, for you, is to face your own son, face to face, frankly without guilt or shame, and tell him how God helped you to become a responsible mother after emancipating you from irresponsible sex. Your son is the creature not of irresponsible sex but of your decision to have him as a gift from God. Irresponsible sex would have made you to commit an irresponsible act of abortion.

It is therefore a mark of dignity to tell your son both your weakness and strengths so that he does not find them out from others. He will forgive whom you have forgiven, love whom you love, and will inherit the hatred of those you have. Better the former than the latter. Dignity is not a nebulous, expansive and endless thing without limits and boundaries. It is what repairs itself after being wounded, and transforms a guilty person into a happy and useful one. In the case of the hypothetical girl, dignity was not found among her teachers, preachers, parents and others who thought that pregnancy was beneath their dignity. The sin of adultery was more compartible with the parental, pastoral, medical and pedagogical views of the world but never the results of it. It was wonderful that dignity led her to hate the sin to forgive the sinners and to love her child. She escaped from the materialism that led others to think to execute an unborn child was the answer to their moral decadence. Out of this moral decay was born a new self-realization, self-respect and self-confidence.

From the above illustrations of how dignity crystallizes itself in a young person we learn that dignity is not a hand-out, inheritance or gift given to child by their parents like property. It is independence and self-reliance gained through behaviour purification and testing to achieve mechanisms of mental adjustment, adoption, conversion and transformation. Dignity does not obligate anybody to choose between good and evil, light and darkness, bad and good, negative and positive, but itself is all that is right, good, positive, light, the antithesis of all wickedness, inequity and inhumanity. In Kenya, our choice is not between dignity and vanity but of the means by which to eliminate vanity, curroption and selfishness. Do not wait to join the police when all policemen cease accepting bribery because the choice is not between you and corrupt policemen but in the methods to eliminate corruption. If Kenya were to be invaded by another country, your moral choice would not be to which country you belong, the invading one or Kenya, but of the weapons to use in combat against the invader. We expect those entrusted with authority in national institutions to use their powers to eliminate the situation that land young people, especially girls in the hands of exploiters. When I came to choosing between good and evil, the parents, teachers, doctors, politicians and pastors who should have helped the hypothetical girl to fight sexual abuse and abortion chose evil.

5.1 THE POWER TO BE HUMAN AND LEARNED

There are teachers and parents who see the world as two things from which to choose dignity, the thing consisting of intelligent students and the thing made of dull ones. Kenya, whose majority of the population consists of children depends on those children for its present and future identity. It should not therefore classify them into two groups, one intelligent and the other stupid. I can recall a teacher who used to encourage the pupils who achieved more marks than others to laugh at them. This teacher used to feel like a paranoid general who saw the school as his empire of academically poor students. This teacher used to eat and drink with the parents of the students who had top marks in his class. He did this so openly that his behaviour amounted to psychological abuse for the parents whose children performed poorly in academic records. Many pupils dropped out of his class to avoid his contemptuous remarks.

The laws by which our teachers rule schools like private empires may be the high standards of cleanliness that discriminate children from poor homes, sportsmanship which may victimize those unable to win cups for their schools, and high marks that humiliate those born with little capacities to understand complicated things. We can teach children without making those less competent than others feel themselves alienated from the school as the greatest agent of socialization and acculturation. School standards should not treat those who fail to achieve them like criminals, outcasts and unwanted.

A teacher represents the government, the family, the industry and the church in the classroom and conveys to the pupils what all these institutions expect from them. A teacher may forget that when he subjects to ridicule, shame and humilation some students by others he is depriving some people the power to be human, self-respectful and self-confident. He is using the classroom and blackboard to create social warfare between future leaders and instituting social classes.

Some teachers have base motives which lead them to use punishment as a means of vengeance against dull and slow learning students and those who brought them into the world. This is because their lack of high academic performance reflects on his professional career and name of the school where he works. The school is a miniature community and a mirror of the brain capacities existing in the nation. The teacher is not God to accept the blame for the way students are talented. Unfortunately some school masters believe that the school is a special and select community of the most brilliant children, from successfully brilliant parents and that the other children are intruders who should have their own school representing their own non-brilliant. Masters like these ignorantly share the concepts of American white racism where neighbourhood schools are supposed to be special organs of a special race. Such concepts are based on a corrupt ideology of wanting to become masters and not human. Dignity is the power to be human.

The teacher therefore, armed with ideas of success in examination as passport to economic, political and social masterdom, wants to eliminate from success those who have no prospects of passing examinations. He succeeds to convince them that they are useless and worthless and that their place is in serfdom. The debilitating effects of our

115

teachers' behaviour, especially when copied and assimilated into the behaviour of their successful students creates merciless dictators who force people to feel that any other job other than the white collar one is beneath human dignity. Brilliant students will leave school with a hostile and oppressive mentality toward their dull classmates and dull classmates graduate with feelings of alienation, inferiority and lack of self-confidence. The purpose of learning experience is to enhance the dignity of the teachers and students without classifying anybody into intellectual categories. The certificate is given not to grade or degrade anyone into vanity, arrogance and rudeness but to recognize the talents God had given to people according to his will.

In a logical class of twenty five students a research exercise revealed the destructive effects of teachers' lack of tolerance toward slow learners in our school system. In six out of the twenty five schools which our theological students attended, those pupils who used to become last in standard one committed suicide before reaching adulthood. In most of these suicidal cases parents were in league with teachers to punish, ridicule, torment and shame those pupils whose performance was a true revelation of the teachers' and parents' professional and genetic capacity. Some of them were given corporal punishment and scolded by teachers and parents in front of other children in school and at home. Before deciding to commit suicide some had made several attempt to run away from home and to drop out of school. Six other victims of academic effort to measure dignity with examination points became last in standard one. These six successfully managed to run away from their homes and schools and ended up as call girls, pick pocketers and parking boys or as failures at the end of their primary education.

Ten others who had become last in standard one but managed to finish standard 8 or 7 failed to achieve any certificate worth notice in any Kenyan employment market. But they were not bothered by lack of employment because they could employ themselves. This happened because the very teachers and parents who had encouraged them to stay in school, despite being last in class, encouraged them to find dignity in themselves and gain self-respect and self-worth. Some of these ten are now useful citizens working for co-operative societies as watchman and in dispensaries as unskilled workers. They can manage their domestic animals and cash crops shambas better than some of those who performed better in examination.

The remaining three out of the twenty five who became last in their class in standard one managed to improve their academic performance as time went on and obtained gods certificates at the end of their primary education. One of them went to high school, the other to technical school where he specialised in carpentry and the other became a successful shopkeeper and farmer. The three felt thankful to their teachers and parents who never gave up on helping them to gain self-confidence and self-respect.

In all the twenty five cases, the community had something to do with determining the death or survival of the children. Where parents and teachers took vengeance against the goods who gave them slow learning children by attacking the children lost the opportunity to become self-reliant, confident and moral in their behaviour. But where the community created self-trust, self-esteem and morality in the slow-learning students it was rewarded by gaining useful members of society.

We cannot therefore admire the teachers who have specialised and mastered in engineering history, physics biology, chemistry, family life, linguistics, anthropology, sociology, theology, child care, medicine, architecture, urban planning, mechanics, law or any other aspect of human education if his studies cause other to lose self-respect, self-confidence, independence and self-reliance. Teacher with high knowledge of their subject matter can use that matter as weapons of destroying students or defending their dignity. If a geographer fails to make dull students draw up a map of Kenya, he can at least make the students understand that the boundaries of Kenya are put there for him to preserve them with his own blood if need be. Just as files that cannot sharpen blunt knives and salt that has lost its saltness are no use a teacher who cannot make good use of a dull and blunt student is of no use. With his own self-confidence, self-reliance and self-trust a teacher can build similar forms of dignity in the pupil. The loss of self-confidence in the young generation arises out of the will of the older generation to dominate rather than communicate. Supposing a teacher who represents the older generation arranges his classrooms in such a way that the child with the least marks sits at the corner of the back row and the one with the most marks sits closes to him at the front row. That distance he puts between himself and the pupil with the least marks will form itself in both his mind and that of student psychically and make that distance permanent behaviour. If that student leaves schools and gets employed as a maid, cook, driver or painter, the same distance will appear between him and his employers and between him and those paid and housed better than him. From the foregoing discussion we can see that a society of adults who lack self-confidence and indpendence communicates the same kind of behaviour to its future generations. Instead of education being a study of the problems a teacher finds in his society, as accepted and put in the curriculum and transmission of problems. But moral, independent and self-reliant behaviour is more a reflection of the dignity of the whole community than it is of the individuals' dignity. Of course, individuals carry the dignity of the community in their actions, beliefs, skills, attitudes, policies, purposes, feelings and character but it cannot form itself automatically without proper nurture, upbringing and education. During childhood a child ought to acquire enough intellectual tools of understanding problems and devising the methods of solving them. It is possible to be learned and be self-reliant without having ever been to a formal school and passed anybody's examination.

The community has no other purpose of existence other than to make its youth learn to be self-reliant, thus, able to govern, support and preserve itself without dependence on its old. Building the youth is the ultimate good of national wealth and power. Without such a goal the nation dies and comes to an end. A self-reliant family, community or nation is the one able to live for more than self-preservation both the ministry to onself and the work of helping others to be self-supporting, self-reliant and independent mark the behaviour of a mature individual, institution or nation. A nation which cannot build itself by building the youth lacks the capacity and ability to have its own culture, tradition and religion and is itself dependent on foreign aid. It has to be aided by others for its behaviour and in its most fundamental goal in life, that is, to pass on dignity to the succeeding generations. Parents, rulers, teachers, nations and societies are not self-reliant until those that they have produced, their successors, are self-reliant. A man who has learnt self-reliance is the one who should teach others what is to be learned, whether one has diplomas and degress or not.

Self-reliance does not therefore mean doing ones own thing or being self-sufficient but being able to use what you have received from God, all the gifts of your life, to serve others. All self-reliant activities are educative, communicative and independent and can therefore be inherited and heired from one generation to another. Anything you have which you have no freedom to give others is not yours but you belong to it. Christ was able to give his life as a sacrifice for our sins because he owed it to nobody, but to himself as a free gift of God. What we deny others death takes away and gives it to them without our consent.

The hungriest and poorest people of the world are those unable to give up their traditions and wisdom and learn new and modern ways of doing things. Modern traditions are modifications, transformations, and alterations of the very old traditions that people surrendered. Those unable to change from their conservative food habits and forming methods die of starvation while those willing to change find their old habits and methods serving in different and renewed forms. Surrendering of cultural habits prevents them from dying because it frees them from slavery and offers them a chance to examine, criticize and recover their value. If the school cannot transform the habits of its children at an early stage and modernize certain useful elements of those habits such school ends up destroying the roots of the childrens' dignity. If children are used to eating their rice milled do not tell them that rice is bad for bodily growth but teach them to eat it unmilled. A school can revolutionize the behaviour of a whole community by transforming the eating habits of its students, teachimg them that breast-feeding is superior to botttle-feeding, eating sukumawiki better than canned foods. In fact, self-reliance in food is crucial to self-reliance in politics. A child, having been taught the value of eating balanced diet from local materials, and this being a part of this curriculum can cause a green revolution and make a nation self-reliant on food. It is due to this kind of resilience in an educational system that a student would develop self-confidence, self-reliance and independence amidst change.

Instead of students deserting their villages after graduation to go and look for non-existent jobs in the city their farming habits can be modified to irrigate, apply fertilizer and insecticides and produce food for both themselves and the village market. A nation cannot divorce from dignity the ability a person, family or country to feed itself. A human being sinks lower than monkeys and all other animals which feed themselves if he cannot feed himself. There is no human dignity whatsoever in any adult who cannot clothe, feed and shelter himself and in that process provide others with similar things, except if he is naturally disabled. The society therefore, organizes itself properly by guaranteeing the coming generations the foundations of self-reliance. There is no point our country making treaties with other countries about freedom of the seas, sharing of international trade, rights of air navigation and national integrity if we cannot guarantee ourselves freedom from hunger.

5:3 THE DIGNITY OF SERVICE TO OTHERS

This leaves us with the questions of what churches and their pastors do to counsel members of the society to bear only those they are capable of giving dignity. Like teachers, pastors spiritual dignity reflects the objective reality of the society to which they belong. Spiritual values are universally acceptable values on the basis of which social laws are made. I find in Kenya laws the ten commandments in their various forms. The laws of "love your neighbour as yourself" are the basis of our traffic code in which our country requires third party insurance. Just as teachers should not treat slow learners as academic waste, pastors should not treat unbelievers as kaffirs, niggers and infidels. Christians around the world whether Baptists, Methodists, Lutherans, Moravians, Presbyterians, Kibanguists, Orthodox, Catholics, Pentecostalists, or Adventists have problems in accepting each other as of equal spiritual dignity. They regard people of different religions as of inferior dignity to their own. This attitude, coupled with racial, class and national arrogance can be a source of civil conflicts which can destroy the dignity of national identity. Human dignity expresses itself in service to mankind and not in grouping and dividing people into opposing groups.

The ethics of a Christian minister should therefore begin as ethics of God's love for the whole world rather than for the part of the world which Christians constitute. The Christian who regards his world as two, one belonging to his church and the other belonging to markets, schools, hospitals and governments makes a mockery of his God whom he addresses as the bearer of the universe. Here a pastor who succeeds in his dignity as a model of human dignity is the one whose likeness is the likeness of God. Jesus' likeness with God was in his capacity to embrace all mankind in his plan of salvation. Dignity, by its very nature as harmonious relations between a person and his environment cannot cause dichotomy between a spiritual and material, physical and mental, and saved and unsaved. This means that a church minister occupies not a church but a social role, not a doctrine of salvation but a spiritual position. His behaviour is independent of his ethnic, national and class identity and yet at the same time belonging to such an identity. The dignity of a pastor is like that of Christ who left heaven without ceasing to belong there and must therefore leave and transcend the parochialism of his local identity. He belongs to both God's kingdom and earthly kingdoms in the sense that he will finally cease being of the earthly kingdoms. Thus one is called to minister to people of different ideologies and traditions some of which are antagonistic to his own without discriminating against them. In our African context it is not advisable for pastors to join

121

political parties or openly support a political candidate. Nevertheless this advise does not apply in cases where it is clear that one has to stand against evil and corrupt politics by supporting positive and constructive politics. Only a timid, ignorant and mean pastor will not stand and be counted to oppose the plan of a political faction to annihilate another. While he should be independent of factional interest and parochial policies, he should, however fight against the transmission and communication of destructive ideologies such as zionism, nazism, apartheid, racism and sexism. He has the ceremonial and ritual power to make him self-reliant and free from ideological controls. A pastor's moral duty is to interpret countemporary problems in relation to higher values of dignity than the global self-interests in economic, trade, military, politics, diplomacy and race. This moral duty compels the member to be a servant of all and a master of none. His dignity is in serving and not in creating an empire for himself. Service determines his morality.

Disorder of any kind is the result of sin and must not be blamed on metaphysical beings. In Kenya, the mass media explains all deaths, even murder by robbers as a call by heavenly forces. The earthly murderers are said to have been agents of the heavenly gods. The media would go even to the extent of attributing the work of Cain when he killed Abel to an assignment by God. Pastors have tended to accept this popular explanation of all deaths as God's call, making it harder for the society to punish careless drivers, apprehend murderers and compensate the families of the bereaved. This, in turn, produces immoral behaviour which destroys social order and national harmony. This kind of immorality is accentuated by the insurance companies who make it harder to receive compensation for human injuries than for vehicle damages after accidents.

The minister works like a member of a big team of workers who include parents, teachers, headmen, police, agronomists, tax gatherers, administrators, accountants, doctors and others whom he must reconcile in order to bring harmony in the community. In his pastoral dignity he becomes directly involved in reconciling a couple experiencing maritial problems. If his aim to preserve marriage does not work he must call lawyers to separate the two people before they kill one another. If divorce is the only way for one to avoid being killed by his partner then the pastor cannot work alone without his team mates, the police, the judges and psychiatrists. Part of the pastors self-reliance is his ability to refer cases to those better trained to handle them than him. Marriage like all other forms of human relationships is a part of the whole human social order in which the right to live is the biggest part. It is good to re-orient those being killed by a disintegrating marriage into new and different forms of human order where life is more comfortable. Disorder, as a form of broken relationship in which violations of personal dignity are the order of the day must not be allowed to continue without protecting the victims. In this sense dignity exists in serving when service is aimed at preserving dignity in both the bodily and social forms. Marriage as a social dignity cannot survive where it ignores the bodily dignity of individuals.

Sometimes a minister finds it impossible to reconcile a child to a family environment where both parents are seeking legal aid to dissolve their union and none wants to retain the siblings. In such a case the minister may opt for having the children given to forster homes or to other families for adoption. Reconciliation for that child, having failed to function within the family, means finding another home where the child will be welcomed and loved. Life belongs to God and dignity to community. This makes it incumbent upon every community to protect the dignity of its living human beings from birth to death, whether it is through education marriage, church, state, or any other system that can rehabilitate victims of immoral behaviour. All institutions are there for service to dignity and must be abolished if their service turns to service to themselves at the expense of human dignity.

The influence of a pastor communicates the will of God in practical service. It can influence the police to treat social marginals as human beings. In 1967 Sam used to be arrested by police for causing problems to motorists. Sam used to earn his living by taxing the drivers whom he helped to find parking spaces in Nairobi a shilling each. This shilling was more income than Sam's father, Kamau, used to earn as profit, selling Chang'aa. Moreover, Sam used to tax the rich directly because he did not attend schools where the government tax money helped other children to receive education. When car owners refused to pay Sam enforced payments by making their car tyres flat. Of course, this was criminal behaviour, and yet, the only way which was left for the rich and the poor in the city to come into contact with each other. A missionary pastor from Canada did a great deal of research on the problems of boys like Sam and helped change our attitude towards them. This helped us to serve Sam at the risk of bypassing the institutions that had failed to serve him.

Today in Kenya pastors are able to provide spiritual dignity to all types of conditions and situations as agents of reconciliation in all aspects of life in homes, schools, factories, firms, barracks, streets, prisons, ships, airlines and wherever people need their services. The fact that they are not effective in some of these areas is due to lack of self-reliance in material resources and equipments. As a member of both national and international team of thinkers, a pastor should remain in his position as an agent of reconciliation in the world. This does not mean isolating himself from the army generals, psychologists, nuclear physicists and genetic engineers, but consulting with them to understand their ethics in relation to national and international issues. If his country wanted to deplete its meagre foreign reserves by buying enriched uranium to manufacture a prestigeous atomic bomb, he must influence physicists to condemn such a programme by suggesting rural electrification as an alternative. This allows the minister to speak on behalf of medicine, politics, law and economics but at the same time retaining his unique dignity of his role as a pastor.

In other words, in an independent country like Kenya, where almost everybody is religious and about eighty per cent are Christians, there is no economic, political, social and cultural self-reliance if spiritual self-reliance is not apart of this independence. Whether a pastor preaches through his church, leadership, Bible study, and prayers, what comes through in his ministry is the significance of human dignity in a self-reliant personality. If people see no formation of independence and confidence in the people to whom the pastor preaches they tend to dismiss this as a relic of colonialism and traditionalism. A pastor's lack of vision may lead him to become a social equipment for pacifying exploited people. Such a kind of "opium of the people" confuses reconciliation with pacification. So, a pastor's duty includes his sisters, members, nuns, elders, deacons and sympathizers in plan of saving the community from adverse conditions. A pastor does not preach in a spiritual vacuum away from the hunger and suffering of his people.

Leaders in any society are likely to attack their people when the people fail to produce the goods, obedience and affection required from them to make leaders feel self-confident, self-worth and self-assured. Teachers, parents and pastors are no different from other leaders in this connection. Leaders blame the led for making them feel beneath dignity and unworthy of leadership. Instead of giving up and handing over to more capable leaders, the leaders who feel inferior and insecure in their social dignity act defensively and therefore very aggressively. A defensive dog that feels cornered can be too dangerous to go nearby. This form of aggression comes from big nations, big men, bosses and husbands who feel slighted by their small neighbours, subordinates and wives. This happens when leadership exists for self-service and not for service to human dignity.

The problems of domination therefore arises out of authority crisis where the leaders feel threatened by their followers. This problem of oppression is acute in schools, offices, and homes where leaders cannot manage their systems properly without the use of force. The threat to authority may be sometimes genuine when a woman may wish to challenge male authority in her marriage. Some women call this women liberation but practise it as domination in reverse, climbing on top of their husbands. Instead of seeking equality with men, which is their divine and natural right, they seek exchange of roles whereby husbands become their subordinates.

In our culture there is nothing like women liberation where a wife is above the dignity of her husband, but only where the dignity of both wife and husband are equal. None, woman or man should be on top of another because both have the same common dignity in whose likeness is the image of God. Both are equal in dignity and humanity. The order in which family government occurs, man as the head and woman as the follower is functional and expedient and does not decrease or increase ones dignity. Our culture is notorious in selling women, in the name of dowry, treating them like investments or commodities. A person may sell several daughters about ten thousand shillings each without paying tax to the government for his income. If dowry is to continue, and it should not, the Income Tax Department must intervene to benefit the public from this lucrative business. Some men, after getting about forty thousand worth of goods, cows, sheep, goats, water tanks, building materials, vehicles and clothes from their daughters intended husbands, all these taxe free, abandon their wives and other children to go to live in the shops making more wealth. Instead of uplifting the standard of living for the mother who cared for the girls while the men roamed about in the village, the lucky father of girls may use the dowry to buy more land to increase labour for the mother or pay dowry elsewhere to acquire himself a younger wife. Dignity in this sense gives way to exploitative behaviour in which men exploit their daughters, their wives and other women to gain social status and prestige.

It is in cases like these where self-reliance for women becomes impossible under archaic and useless traditions. Dignity requires the equal participation of all people in determining their lives and controlling the conditions that govern their future. There wre times when certain of our traditions, like that of throwing away twins, babies whose upper teeth showed first and dowry had a function of preserving society and stabilising the family, but now to perpetuate such things is to destroy the very essence of human value that our traditions intended to protect.

Finally the question of dignity and self-reliance is the question of what kind of life carries dignity. If dignity is the love of life for its own sake does this mean that when life suffers too much and can no longer sustain itself independently and naturally we must allow mercy killing? Mercy killing is not necessary for human beings under all circumstances. At the same time, however, when a person reaches such a poor state of health that his like is kept by artificial means, his body lying in bed without visible movements and his mind unaware of his environment, no communication between the outside world and him is possible, that person loses the behaviour of dignity. We may pray for him, give him medicine and do all the surgeries at our scientific and technological disposal but the person fails to respond. This condition lasts for days, weeks and months. The man would have died weeks ago if we did not interfere with nature to stop it taking its course. But due to our fear of bad publicity, that we did not take care of the sick, we can preserve the sick mechanically with artificial means, under intensive and expensive care. We should know that the same Lord who gave life, he takes away and that those who have parted with their earthly dignity have the opportunity of having glory in heaven. The same God who gave man the potential capacity to have dignity on earth will crown him with glory. In heaven dignity will become glory.

Human dignity and human body, while continuous with each other, these become separable at death. In some cultures, as in the old Egyptian civilization the bodies of kings were preserved in better conditions than the ones of living kings because the idea of separating dignity from the body was unacceptable. This idea of dignity in dead bodies existed among the Jews who carried the bones of Jacob and other Patriarchs with them and in the Christian doctrine of resurrection of the body. But this is not a justification for stopping people like Tito of Yugoslavia and Generalismo of Spain from dying. The Yugoslavia and Spanish government tried their best to prolong life for these leaders beyond their natural ability to continue living. Perhaps they feared them dying and going to hell.

Nature, death being natural, does not contradict the miracle of the resurrection of the body if the body means some orderly form of existence. Only that we do not know the form in which resurrected bodies shall appear. Our present concern is that our earthly existence must be in the form of self-conscious and self-reliant behaviour. The quality of life in which people enjoy their existence, are happy with their social image and confident of themselves should be the goal of medical care. Medical knowledge should not be exploited by politicians and generals to have their own lives prolonged mechanically for reasons inimical to human dignity. If the doctors and relatives of the patient feel morally wrong to switch off the machines that maintain the patient alive like a vegetable they can refer the decision to the High Court to determine whether the patient life is worth being maintained mechanically.

Ours is a global battle in which all people should be armed with love for one another to preserve the dignity of each other. We live in a world where inter-dependence and partnership are necessary among equals but not among slaves and masters, conquerors and colonized and superior and inferior. For some of us self-reliance is a lonely struggle to sustain our unique nature of being human in a world where the majority are inhuman. We have to love our neighbours in the same way we love ourselves which means that we must struggle hard to break the barriers that make us satisfied with only our dignity.

By our love we shall know that others have human dignity whose independence from us makes them and us inter-dependent. This love is what makes us feel self-confident when faced with the overwhelming forces of evil that would like to destroy our freedom to like the unlikeable, help the ungrateful and rescue the suffering. Our moral, independent and self-reliant behaviour is itself dependent on the love of God who requires us to sacrifice ourselves for others the way he sent his son to do.

CHAPTER 6
DIGNITY AND SELF-INTERESTS
6:1 SUBDUING GROUP, TRIBAL AND RACIAL SELF-INTERESTS

This far we have seen human dignity as the moral worth of being human, and not excluding the material worth of things by which a person maintains himself alive. While human dignity consists of being, as opposed to having, it includes the resources and relations by which being sustains itself. This being is both spiritual and physical and exists in a natural social and territorial context known as the nation. The human body which carries life and its dignity needs material and intellectual resources to maintain it.

It is at this secondary level of having things, rather than on the primary level of being human, where belongs self-interests. Self-interests are good when united with other's interests to form common interests and bad when fulfilled at the expense of others. Self-interests, in so far as, and as far as, they cannot be integrated into others interests to form common interests are destructive of the relations by which societies maintain themselves and lead to the disintegration of human dignity. While a nation is a self-interest group, a nation which pursues its self-interest without limits must go to war with others.

While dignity seeks the continuity of life for its own sake self-interests can lead individuals, states and nations to wipe out others or be wiped out in pursuance of empty pride. Self-interests can create competetive and rival interests amongst brothers and sisters. I know of a clan whose families destroyed each other trying to settle the question of which family has the legitimate rights to graze and cultivate the scarce clan land. The question of dignity is therefore related to the one of self-interests in that while dignity deals with life itself, self-interests deal with the means and methods of keeping oneself alive. The issue of who has access to, owns, or controls grains, water and milk becomes therefore the fundamental issue of dignity itself, thus, human existence.

Such things as political power, allocation of goods and services, cannot be left at the mercy of self-interests, private ownership and personal possession because this can have adverse effects on the right of others whose self-interests are excluded. Common interests as represented in a democratically organized society are the best way of guaranteeing everybody some basic means of existence. Any human organization which guarantees joy, respect and livelihood to some at the exclusion of others destroys the common dignity of all. A nation cannot school books and pencils to pupils, fertilizer and seeds to farmers, and medicine to the sick and continue to have national dignity. Such a nation would suffer the fate of other nations with corrupt regimes that are governed by parasitical rulers. A good state should not have self-interests whatsoever other than the security and welfare of the nation, thus, the people.

The most troublesome factions of self-interests are the owners of property who love having for the sake of having because this creates divisions between themselves and the have-nots. Those who hold the means of survival, individually or collectively but deny others participation in the production, distribution and use of those means form the distinctive self-interests that are detrimental to the peace, love, unity and integrity of their country. Their self-interests are conflicting with those whose self-interest result to jealousy, hatred and bitterness. The possession of property or power without creating the conditions in which others can benefit arouses suspicion, fear and antagonism against the possessors. The monopoly of power and resources is the extreme form of self-interest which undermines human love, respect and confidence, and other characteristics of dignity. Without the sharing of resources through taxation, harambee, wage-employment and public services a nation can easily have two hostile self-interest groups, the "haves" and "have-nots".

The work of bringing together the various self-interests and uniting them to form common interests, thus, subduing the principal of having under that of being, is the fundamental task of modern national governments. It is the duty of every national state to recognize what are the common interests of all members of a given community and to guarantee them the means of satisfying them. The fact that even nations act according to self-interests make it necessary to have an international body that regulates national self-interests. Common interests themselves do not depend on the morality of rulers, nor on the virtues of the bodies regulating them, but on the rights of all individuals who have surrendered self-interests to form common interests. In the case of democracy, voters are the ones responsible for the maintenance of common interests. Governments themselves, whether democratic, dictatorships, military, monarchies, imperial, colonial or communist, are tempted to have self-interests separate from those of the governed. This is why we think that frequent local and national elections are essential to common interests in order to remove from power those whose self-interests are antithetical and unsymphathetic to those of the population. Kenyans do not only need elections in order to rule themselves but in order that those who rule them may not misrule. A state may detain, punish or hand those who threaten and undermine the interests of the nation and its people without provoking revolt or mass protests, but may not do the same without public uproar if people think of that as being done for the selfish interests of those in power.

Although social and political institutions do not operate on the principles of Ten Commandments, but on the basis of their founders' self-interests, they require ethics, constitutions, treaties, vows and other helpful standards that put limits to their self-interests. Left alone without moral laws some military and political organizations will use bullets, teargas, napalm and nuclear weapons to impose their interests on the people. Obviously, self-interests, whether of individuals, or organizations such as multinational corporations must be subjugated by common agreements to common interests. This is what makes it necessary for the registration of any organization so that it does not infringe on the interests of other organisations.

Human dignity therefore finds fulfilment in the free and voluntary association of individuals to form common laws by which they protect their common good at the expense of minority or even majority self-interests. Even such things as national development become harmful to human dignity when the construction of roads, schools or hospitals is for the benefit of a majority faction in society without due regard to the interests of affected minorities. Our laws in Kenya have put into account that individuals who suffer, lose property or experience hardship due to confiscation of their rights, for public interests, should be fairly compensated. Since Kenya regards wild animals as a common national resource, it has made legal provisions for paying to owners the damages caused to their crops by wild animals. The individual farmer's interests are taken care of by the interests of the rest of the society which wants to preserve wild life. It is human dignity when a nation of 22 million people can say sorry to one person and redress him for damages.

There are no personal interests that do not relate to other's interests and no national interests that do not affect international ones. Human dignity therefore cannot find satisfaction in isolation from others without giving rise to the violation of other's dignity the result of which may be military, civil and trade conflicts. When I talk of self-interests, I mean my share of the air, seas, space land, energy and food with over five other billion people who have similar claims to mine by virtue of their existence in this planet. I may differ from others in my identity as a black man or woman from Kenya but differences in traditional, cultural, racial and national backgrounds should not affect our common human need for the means of survival. This does not mean that in common national interests there exists no self-interests at all. Self-interests continue to exist in common national and international systems of interests as a part of self-determination. Self-determination is not possible without one being sure that his rights are taken care of and protected together with others' rights. The nation as the body which represents the self-determination of a given population permits the self-interests of everyone in that population to appear in its policies, programmes and plans for development but at the same time overcoming the antagonisms and separateness between them. Human dignity therefore seeks satisfaction in self-interests being realized in common interests. The goal and objectives of self-interests are attained through the attainment of those of the common interest. In this case a husband does not seek satisfaction from his wife without at the same time seeking to satisfy her. Hence common interests are mutual self-interest. We must recognize that despite Kenya being a melting pot of many racial ethnic and personal self-interests before these can cool thoroughly to form one common interest it will take decades. You are not going to make European girls marry Asian boys overnight or make Asian boys marrying African girls tomorrow. One will also find it difficult to force the economically advantaged groups to form common interests with the less advantaged ones. Under the existing cover of equality under the law and the protection of private property, one discovers racial and class groups still separated from others by their differences in origin, and attitudes. This is the behaviour of some citizens of Kenya who having developed superiority complex during colonial times try to have no other contact with others except in the factories, shops and streets. This is less than national or human dignity because the need for each other is money in an employer-employee relationship and not for common identity. The Bible says that patience is one of the fruits of the Holy Spirit, and should apply in Kenya where everybody must tolerate the other.

We therefore need to define the qualification for human dignity given our different self-interests and considering that it is not the wisdom of rulers, the talent of scientists, or the morality of preachers that will bring the people together but taking care of their self-interests. Partly as a result of the gospels own insitence on human dignity as a gift of God you may find nations who have accepted all people are created equal. But the gospel itself, especially in America and South Africa and in the relationship between Israelis and Palestinians can be misused by some to justify self-interests at the exclusion of others' interests. The Gospel is therefore not able to bring people together without the struggle of colonized and exploited people to put into effect what it says. The United

133

Nations regards as perpetrators of mischief and injustice nations that permit the self-interest of some to undermine self-interests of other.

But no matter what man does to liberate himself from any manner of indignity, injustice or threat to his life he rises above the means used and the gain. Man makes himself and determines his own destiny and frees himself from his successes or failures of today in order to remake himself anew tomorrow . His dignity is not a slave to any of its previous stages of growth and development. Dignity never sinks to the level of being a product or a commodity. The fruits of dignity thus, love, peace, unity, intergrity and hope have their meaning not in books philosophies, constitutions and doctrines that men have produced but in real human interests where peace or unity comes in sharing "Ugali", bed and sorrow.

One can do things and produce things that can reinforce as well as negate his dignity like the people who spend all their lives accumulating property for its own sake and die disatisfied and poor in their souls. *The total sum of what a man produces in this world, money, commodities, influence, fame and ideas does not amount to his dignity.* This is why everybody should live and die humble.

Unlike domestic animals whose value is measured by the products of their bodies and labour, the value of human beings is more than in their bodies and work. Unlike dogs whose value is measured by their ability to provide their masters with security, horses whose value is measured by their ability to transport and entertain their owners, and oxen whose value is measured by their ability to pull ploughs and yield meat, *human value is beyond any known measurement of value.* In fact, if we were to apply traditional scales of measuring the value of human beings, some people's bodies would fetch less money than cows, pigs and rabbits. While these animals share interests in neither the profit of their work nor in the sale of their meat, human beings. except when colonized, enslaved and opressed, do not engage in activities in which they have no interests in the results. To subject one person to the self-interest of another and force him participate in activities for which he has no interest is the worst form of greedy self-indulgnece, selfishness, degeneracy and immorality because, it is using a fellow human being like an animal. *Hence, human dignity is the antithesis of any use of one person by another for interests not shared in common.* It is the antithesis of being in the hands of another like a consumable and expendable item. Until all in a group agree to surrender self-interests to form common-interets nobody should surrender his other than if called by God to do so.

It is a lamentable chapter of our history that Kenya used to belong to international economic sphere of interests in which our fathers and mothers were sold like goods during the slave trade, suffered the costs of European degeneracy during the second and First World Wars, and inherited the bankruptcy of capitalism during the fall of the British Empire. Even today we belong to the same international systems of foreign self-interests which are destroying our natural environment without at the same time allowing us to profit from the wealth derived from that environment. Though labour and taxation laws have tried their best through wage guidelines and taxation of profits to benefit the country, the International Monetary Fund and World Bank continue to serve western self-interests by demanding these to be relaxed. The self-interests of foreign profit seeks to produce social, psychological, political and cultural conditions that make the exploited dependent on exploiters for essential goods and services. Lies that the self-interests of a dominant nation, race, class or elite are the only holy ones and that those of the poor are dangerous to law and order end up destroying the moral order upon which dignity for both rich and poor depends. People should never surrender their self-interests to others with whom they share no common interests. Common interest is a compound of the self-interests of those who benefit from the compound.

Many European theorists, especially colonial writers would like us to believe that the Africans of pre-slave trade and pre-colonial times had no self-interests of any kind. Without wasting our time refuting their arguments, we can derive our ethics of dignity from the present conditions without returning to the primordial conditions of traditional innocence that never was; not to a time of communal life that is no more. Our past, has no other relevant meaning other than that which it receives from us, here and now. From my own ethnic background I have received patience and endurance for my dignity and from the corporate national life received dynamism and vitality. While it is impossible to detach myself from my African traditional background when it comes to my struggle against alien interests I need to understand the theology, psychology, politics, sociology, economics and technology by which these interests influence mine.at my expense. The most sinful people are not those who enslaved and colonized my ancestors but those who having been entrusted with my religion, education and morality convert these into instruments of furthering their self-interests at my expense.

The most miserable people are not those who steal by burglarizing and robbing others by use of violence, but those who are discovered taking advantage of commonly held interests to satisfy self-interests. Civil wars are worse than international wars because they are fought by people who feel their trust betrayed by others. This is the problem facing South Africa where people of one national interest divide that interest into sub-interests giving the majority blacks less than the minority whites.

In Kenya, we have not reached a high degree of institutional maturity in which conflicting self-interests can compete with one another without this disrupting the social order that sustains common dignity. One cannot preserve himself in ways that threaten the self-preservation of others without provoking them into violence. Kenya is not unique in this feeling that all tribal self-interest groups, parties, classes and factions are enemies of one another. All tribal and group self-interests should be banned or nationalized.

You cannot have exclusive racial or ethnic self-interests without causing those excluded to have their own exclusive self-interests opposed and antagonistic to your own. Exclusive Asian or European sports clubs, businesses or schools may one day cause a crisis like the one Asians experienced in Uganda in 1971.

In America and Britain where ethnic differences are diffused and the governments under the control of racial majority, self-interests can survive without the fear of internal challenge. In countries where the strength of collective action in the government is very developed, the integration of contradictory and opposite interests is very old, some degree of selfishness is allowed, people can tolerate the self-interests of one group to dominate theirs. The British Feudal aristocracy was able to rule United Kingdom and to maintain the empire for centuries without the support of the middle class because it allowed middle class capitalism to make profits. But when the middle class realized that capitalism in the world can succeed without imperialism it discarded the idea of the empire. Once the British middle class learned from the examples of America that capitalism does not rise or fall with the specific forms of government in power, and that independent countries like India and Nigeria can be exploited by capitalists more profitably than colonies, it started to liberalize its attitude toward overseas possessions. The middle class had capitalism as its distinctive self-interests while the feudalism had the glory of power as its distinctive self-interests. This tolerance of two distinct self-interests toward each other lasted until the middle class had secured its interests in the colonies through its own independent networks of industrial, commercial, financial and psychological controls and in collaboration with the colonized people. While feudalism exploited colonies without the consent of colonized people capitalism exploits independent countries with their consent. If we refuse to be exploited the French and British armies will receive American assistance to return.

At our present stage of political and economic development it is almost impossible for two classes of self-interests to achieve national collaboration. In our one party system of government, those who miss their chance now lack the hope of getting it tomorrow. So, we have inherited a national system of administration of human interests in which we are engaged in the enormous task of working as one interest despite being many interests. This appears unhealthy but nevertheless is orderly.

:1 MERGING SELF-INTERESTS INTO COMMON INTERESTS

Dignity therefore leads to the acceptance of other's interests without classifying them into racial, ethnic or class categories. The basic premise of dignity as a system of human values is self-respect for everybody, which means talking with your enemies and helping them when in need. This fundamental promise is clearly articulated in the story of the Good Samaritan. The eyes of dignity can see the value of the other, recognize his needs and deal with his problems before knowing his class, tribe, sex, passport, identity card, insurance certificate, academic credentials, hereditory background or social status. When Americans were in need of the Russians to defeat Hitler they forgot ideological self-interests and joined hands to achieve common goals. The same attitude should prevail even when the common goal is not to defeat a common enemy but on matters of nation building. In Kenya where Asian and European minority groups have resisted to have economic, cultural and social interaction with Africans common interests are harder to achieve than between Africans themselves.

The way to achieve unity in pluralism and divergent is not therefore to supress others interests but to incorporate them into your own. The choice to accept other's self-interests or reject them is the choice between peace and war, between death or life. The longer any group remains at low level of consciousness in its desire to merge its interests with others' interests the greater the violence that group will suffer if the war of interests begins. The time when history consisted óf elites ruling other groups through creeds, customs and intimidations without caring for their interests is gone. The time has come, for even those claiming neutrality, disinterestedness and immunity between self-interest to know that theirs is also a group self-interest. The psychological state of every man or nation is that "we pretend neutrality in order to benefit from their war of self-interests." There was a family in which children used to enjoy their parents fighting because they could choose which one to give sympathy and get paid for it. In the end both parents ended their marriage feeling that their children were double-dealers. So, if you happen to see a group of people engaged in a fight if you do not intervene in peace-making. Kenya Asians should help rather than take advantage of low degree of unity amongst Kenyans of different tribal backgrounds by availing their business experience and expertise.

Dignity is total involvement in peace-making to preserve order and security. People feel their dignity strengthened, affirmed and increased when others are engaged in their struggle to survive ulterior motives and without strings attached.

They also love others to join them in national efforts in the process of which everybody shares setbacks, defeats and frustrations as well as victories. There is no dignity watching others suffer or harvesting where one had not sown, coming to share success with the people with whom you had not faced death together. Some citizens of Kenya live in groups that experience periodical famine, disease epidemics and high unemployment while others who benefited from racialism during colonial times share resources with them.

Self-interests, narrowly defined are attitudes and activities in which exclusive groups like to gain theirs and other's share of benefits while at the same time avoiding to share the cost and loses. When self-interests collapse into selfishness one becomes a grabber of others property, money, power and positions. In every righteous man, and in the life of all saints, there is this necessary conflict between dignity and self-interests in which dignity sacrifices self-interests to form

139

common interests. To the extent to which I as a church minister need shelter, food and clothing, for myself and my family, I must have self-interests. At the same time my own dignity has crystallized into rendering these self-interests a contribution to common interests. This is why I must speak the truth even if it means being crucified and leaving my family without help, under God's care. Jesus Christ himself became man in order to experience self-interests like us, so that by overcoming his, he can help us overcome ours. Therefore, self-interests do not necessary lead to greed, selfishness and sin and can bring blessings when merged with those of others. Only life should be pursued for its own sake. The co-operative movement in Kenya is a good example of how self-interests of workers can be merged to become common interests.

When one ruling elite excites his followers to demand the consumer, commercial and industrial resources belonging to the constituency of another, such as elite pursues self-interests without minding the self-interests that led others to produce those resources. Self-interests, in this selfish sense may elevate social economic differences into ethnic, racial and class conflicts. There are other Kenyans who feel that Asians and Europeans should transfer some of their means of production to Africans to achieve racial equality without saying that the Kikuyu, Luo, Kamba, Kalenjin and Taita should do the same to Samburu, Turkana and Pokot to achieve ethnic equality. What they advocate would destroy the self-interests of Kenyan economy upon which our social, business, political and national infrastructures are built. The disproportionate property in the hands of privileged groups in the result of past inequalities that cannot be resolved by destroying advantaged groups but by political reorganization and economic transformation of the whole national economy. Transfer of property from one group to another does not create or add property. But existing property can be highly taxed to help generate property for those without any.

One cannot punish the privileged because he wants to reward the underprivileged but must change the whole social organization that creates the two conflicting self-interests. The self-interests of the slave and the master to eliminate each other are as unjust as maintaining slavery and masterdom. The point at which dignity comes in is where the slave and the master change their relationships completely so that their separate roles and exclusive positions are abolished for ever. Exchanging of positions and transfer of power and property among unequal races, tribes and classes does not remove inequality but rather legitimizes it. The issue in Kenya has been how to abolish such things as Asian, European or African business, residential areas, schools and social clubs and replace them with national ones. This is what President Moi did with tribal football clubs, land buying companies and societies when he came into power. This action of our President has helped to speed up national integration and identity.

Self-interests broadly defined, therefore must be connected with common interests irrespective of which group originated them. If the idea of piped water in every kitchen originates from women as a self-interest group such a good idea should become a national interest because even men need water in their homes. To have a tarmac road in a tea growing area, a coffee factory in a coffee plantation or a blinds' school at Thika is as national as the government iself and has nothing to do with parochial or regional self-interests. Where something is or is being done is not as crucial to human dignity as to who benefits. Things that are fed by truth, honesty and integrity as and have national availability liberate a country from disunity, disorders and violence. In a free, just and democratic society, the ultimate object of all government, business, industrial, religious and social workers is to serve the nation in a way that benefits all. In the process, the ultimate goal of service is to make life enjoyable, respectable and holy, for it is life that carries dignity and not the things we own.

Finally give people all your possessions, guns, money, homes, land and technology and they will turn against you as a fickle, cowardly, foolish and useless leader who cannot give them enough. But invest the same 'possessions in national development to help themselves and they will thank you for giving them freedom, work, justice, peace and love: dignity. They will offer to you their sons and daughters over and above recording your name together with the names of heroes like Jesus, Gandhi and Kenyatta. Let the people know that their lives are worth more than the certificates they received in schools, the wages they obtained from their employers and the ranks of power occupancy, and they will love you, thus, give themselves to you in exchange of having given yourself to them, life for life, and never life for things.

Dignity is in life and not in things. This is what distinguishes dignity from self-interests which are in things. This is why when we speak of respect, esteem and confidence we are addressing ourselves to people and when we talk of interests we are addressing ourselves to things. When we meet others we should therefore esteem, respect and trust them before categorizing them as means to an end. Self-interest is a relation of man to things he wants to use. If others want to use the same things consent to share them is common interests. This is essential to peace, love and unity.

Our aim in the foregoing chapter has been to erase in human minds the use of others solely for the pleasure other than their own. It has been also to correct the distorted view of life that the have-nots are less dignified than the haves and that the haves are more human than the have-nots. Self-interests should be pursued as common interests, not vested interests. Dignity is contentment with what and who we are and not with what we have. There is no amount of things that can satisfy and fulfil the meaning human dignity. Dignity levels down the material and power world into something temporal, small and of no consequence. One of the benefits of accepting Christ in my life was the feeling that I now owned the one who owned me, the one above the universe, the one who shall destroy the popes, bishops, presidents, kings, emperors, and angels who pursue their self-interests at the expense of other's. This made my dignity to have jurisdiction over my self-interests.

In the next chapter we shall see how dignity liberates men and women from traditional systems and helps them create a new order of freedom from worries into freedom to enjoy life as a gift from God.

CHAPTER 7
HUMAN DIGNITY AND COMMON INTERESTS

7.1 COMMON INTERESTS LEAD TO NATIONAL INTEGRATION

Human dignity transforms self-interests into common interests. This transformation of self-interests into common interests is the highest form of cultural development because it elevates people above their individual, personal and private interests. It helps people to surrender themselves to a corporate and collective history of the communities to which they belong. Human dignity entrusts life to national agencies, organizations and institutions that are more fit and capable of preserving it than the tribes, clans and castes to which their ancestors belonged. Except in slavery, colonialism and prison where self-interests are destroyed and eliminated, in free systems and relationships all human self-interests become the necessary raw material for forming common interests.

A parent, affected by the ignorance of his children would be destroyed by it unless there were schools which were more specialized than parents in handling educational interests. Similarly, the church, mosque or temple takes care of spiritual and social needs and problems of their members better than individuals and families in dealing with certain levels of educational and spiritual needs. That is why we have left the state to run some institutions like universities. There are therefore some self-interests that go beyond the capacity of the individuals, families, communities, districts and provinces to handle and must be surrendered to national or international institutions for better management and solutions. African countries must regard as common interests issues like locust control, desertification and communication. To go to sleep or to work in a peaceful manner some people, and even nations need to share the responsibilities of peace and security with their neighbours. The responsibility of maintaining dignity requires personal and national independence and inter-dependence.

Kenyan women know that their dignity does not consist of acquiring more recipes, cosmetics, fashions and feminity to satisfy their male counterparts but in forming common interests with men. Their men cannot survive on sports, politics business, religion, power, fame and intellect without forming common interests with their women to promote family and national interests. Both the family and the government, in Kenya have become identical institutions which cannot survive without the survival of all the interest parties, women, men, children, adults, old and everybody. This is why the nation as much as the family, exists for the common interests of self-perpetuation. Just a family survives by ensuring the survival of its members, which is the moral foundation of the society, the nation preserves itself .by preserving the families. The government is there to ensure that nobody pursues self interests that are in conflict with common interests and everybody preserves himself only by methods that assist the self-preservation of others. This is why the state has the responsibility of helping children whose parents are plagued with alcoholism, absenteeism, crime, bankruptcy and other psycho-social problems. Some human problems, though affecting an individual, must be taken over by the community or state where the individual and his family show signs of defeat. The state should not allow people to do away with their own lives or families to eliminate themselves. It has to intervene to save the situations. I believe that this kind of intervention should be extended to affect those nations whose government take care of the self-interests of some tribes, races, classes or castes creating common interests as in Southern Africa. An international body must intervene on behalf of dignity to save the victims of others self-interests. But there are times when two categories of self-interests can satisfy each other without common interests like when a patient offers money to a doctor and the doctor offers medicine. But the state which trains and licences the doctor caters for the interest for both.

This is why all self-interests, no matter how narrow or

broad must be licensed by the state in order to operate on the basis of respect for others' rights. A society is not a society of individuals living in it but of their total interests. In human dignity I am my brother's keeper. In dignity I can recognize the problems of a wounded neighbour because his wounds are what all his neighbours share with him in common. If his wounds were to change into a nice tea drinking and goat meat-eating party, even his enemies would hide amongst other neighbours to have a share. Personal animosities disappear when others invite us to share in their success because we hated them because of our self-interests. Just as we are happy when others transform their self-interests to common interests and make their achievements available to us, we should be happy surrendering our moral, emotional and material concerns to others. This surrendering of self-interests should not be done by individuals to other individuals but to an organized body or institution in which all are represented.

The family is the primary institution, which just as much as the state handles self-interests more effectively and efficiently than individuals. It provides greater happiness, protection and opportunities to its members than an individual pursuing them on his own. Unlike some animals whose calves are born almost capable of behaving like adults and fetching for their own food, human beings need about sixteen to twenty years of dependence before they can stand on their own. Children have interests or needs, but no self-interests. A person has self-interests when he owns something or can compel others to give him what they own. There are no self-interests without power to negotiate, bargain, exchange or trade with others for what one has. There was a time when women were supposed not to have self-interests and could not sign contracts, bank money, vote or pay taxes. Slaves were equally regarded as people with needs for security, food, shelter and health but without self-interests. Today only prisoners, drunkards and children whose dignity forfeits self-interests for others to take care of. I used to live in a family where my grandfather used to come home totally drunk at midnight, and wake everybody up including his small grandchildren. The family lacked the moral courage to limit and control him and therefore left him free like it left natural epidemics, floods, debts and famine over which it had lost control. While there are some juvenile, sick and abnormal human beings whose interests must be met without anything being expected from them. Our aim is to make people normal self-reliant, independent and free so that they have something to sacrifice or pay for what they get from others.

Consequently, our families, institutions and nation can thrive in dignity where every man and woman has self-interest in common interest. Without self-interest in national interest it is easy to become a traitor. One must have a state in the system in order to defend it. Throughout their lives normal human beings are sure of themselves as not self-sufficient in everything. Even a king has to surrender some of his privacy to have a bodyguard, driver and cook besides sharing some of his property to pay their salaries. In national policies, common interests may be national goals, projects and defence. Even at national level you need control to avoid having unsurrendered self-interests like those of Judas who betrayed the common cause.

Without dignity and national identity as discussed in chapter one and two of this book, the police, doctors, traders, teachers, parents, civil servants, politicians and magistrates will continue using home, schools, administration and courts to enrich themselves.

Behind such psychological and social unity that we shall common interests we find networks of men and women who have surrendered their lives to serve others. Such people realize that individuals are not made to control floods, epidemics and wars but to organize thousands of people and train them to act together in a harambee spirit.

Kenyans also needs men and women in whose minds common interests have become self-interests. The president of a country is a woman or man who has surrendered her or his self-interests to the country in order to take the common interest of the whole population as her or his self-interests. The government, industry, commerce and social organizations are full of leaders whose positions do not allow them to pursue self-interests in private or while on duty. Their behaviour, attitude and decisions have major consequences. A bishop or District Commissioner cannot neglect his family and excuse this as private self-interest. As a church minister, I have found that my failure to act, to make decisions or respond to social issues, is itself an act of betrayal to common interests greater than things I have done. We Kenyans have now achieved such a high degree of common interest that we no longer can leave matters of health, morality, wealth, power and planning to private individuals. We must recognize the need of men and women, full of dignity and its virtues, to occupy the strategic command posts of our social structures in which have now concentrated the effective means of power and means of existence.

Given the complexity and magnitude of common interests in Kenya the president of the country and his decision-making machineries of advisers, cabinet ministers, military heads, permanent secretaries, parliamentarians, administrative commissioners and directors are among those in our national establishments who should resign, or forced to do so, if discovered to have any remnants of self-interest in their offices. Jesus taught love for the people not only as the power by which lovers can break the boundaries of self-interests and behave like children of one father, but as the power by which the interests of those loved become of the lover. In this sense a leader must love his country and its people so much that his interests are those of his country and people. This is what patriotic spirit means.

In Kenya, where some ethnic and racial groups have greater economic and political advantages than others, leaders from there can break the mental limitations of their followers that prevent integration into common national interests. Having become national to their positions as parliamentarians, civil servants, professionals and enterpreneurs, the elite can provide the example of having given up tribal and parochial interests in exchange of national ones. Dignity is an inclusive and universal human capacity to rise above ones own personal, clan, class and sectional interst to accomodate those of others. Instead of fighting for self-interest, men of dignity join forces to form the highest unified command possible.

147

To create moral, intellectual and emotional conditions in which people see their nation as an enlarged family where their interests are ministered requires personnel in churches, government and other institutions with national self-confidence. Without personnel dedicated and devoted to common interests people are likely to feel alienated by their leaders and made hostile to these national institutions. The presence of dignity in any public institutions is noticeable from the way workers in these institutions have their ethnic, class, rural, urban, academic, racial or clan interests been transformed to accommodate those of the "clients" and "customers". Indeed what we call clients, customers and subjects are the pillars of virtually all healthy and demoractic institutions.

From the example of our African grandparents, whose land, property and culture we have inherited we have learned to find fulfillment in the open and generous action of giving pleasure to a person outside our families, clans, language, and traditions. These welcomed the missionaries from whom we learned that we too can benefit by receiving from those we welcome into our struggle for existence.

7.2 NATIONAL CUSTODIANS OF COMMON INTERESTS

The self-sacrificial and self-giving character of dignity that we have discussed above finds fulfillment in serving others without ever making a demand or placing restriction upon the one served. I have discovered that the early nationalists succeeded to win peoples hearts because they had open and loving interests in people and not in the things people gave them. In fact they worked hard, night and day, without ever receiving or demanding material wages and risked their lives for others to get independence. Kenyatta's moral dignity was even higher than that of the priests and catechists of his time. In comparison with him the British settlers, governors and soldiers had no dignity. Mahatma Gandhi had a dignity similar to that of Kenyatta, a dignity more powerful than that of British kings, generals and bishops. These men, with their dignity, overcame the power of western Christianity and civilization which tried to use them as tools of capitalism and imperialism. The other day I listened to a man who accepted being used by western Christendom as an instrument of oppressing his own people condemning those who refused to become tools, saying "My education in England has gained me my wealth, prestige and power in my country". He went on to boast of his European-made "dignity" by castigating people educated in local universities as fools. I wondered what would be the attitude of this gentlemen toward the peasants of Kenya who never had the opportunity to go beyond primary school education.

It is unfortunate that it is the men without dignity who appear to have it due to dignity being associated with their positions, possessions and certificates. Such people tend to be brutal, cruel and wicked because they cannot recognize the dignity of others below their social and economic positions. They have so much arrogance that humility becomes a rare commodity in their offices. Their character is the worst enemy of common interests despite their education elevating them into employment as custodians of national interests.

There should be methods of measuring the amount of human dignity, respect, esteem and trust for others that one has before engaging him as a custodian of common interests. Despite the fact that self-interests will lead people to seek important positions in society, through bribery, corruption, military force or academic merits, a criterion for dignity should be established to guage how human are the candidates of such positions. Doctors and lawyers in Kenya do have moral codes to guide their practises which lack in many other areas of public service. Without moral guidance certain individuals can ruin their own lives more than others. I heard of a man, who after many years of service in the government attempted suicide because the things he had earned were put under auction notice. Had he earned love from the people he would have sought and received sympathy from them. Men who like to spend most of their lives eating, drinking and socializing with people like gregarious animals do, on the basis of class, rank and status die without leaving a true mark of friendship, companionship and intimacy in the world. They

149

die and are buried without leaving behind them true disciples.

The whole ethics of work and reward in Kenya is moving toward such a materialistic condition that unless arrested our institutions will end up being the tools of those in power to protect themselves from the people. As long as we continue to make a student feel that studies without gaining a certificate are useless, a worker to believe that wages are more important than the service rendered, then we are emphasizing the aspect of self-interests than of common interests. Instead of life having meaning and purpose in the harmonious relationship in society, striving for personal gain makes the worker feel guilty of producing more than he is paid for. But if somebody did some work like stealing, robbing and barglarising others, contrary to him dignity and incongruous to common interest, works hard to avoid detection by police he becomes a hero eligible for a position in parliament, appointment to head a statutory board, and consecration to become bishop. It appears that it is becoming harder to reach the top of organizations based on common interests unless one goes through the route of base self-interests.

Yet, there still remains fulfillment and joy in the work that affirms human dignity where one rises to the top or not. Man should find satisfaction as a farmer co-operating with nature, moisture, air and worth to make the earth produce food for the community, as a scientist operating nature, elements, atoms, compounds and energies to produce goods that make life in a society easier, as a doctor manipulating nature bodily tissues, drugs and organisms to reduce causes of suffering and death in the nation, as an organizer teaching, governing, preaching and doing other things to make society orderly and happy. The worker should feel happy in his role as a shoe-shinner, street vendor, private soldier and house maid because he or she spends life where he or she earns the means of existence. A young man will fight for his country not because of the monetary reward but because he believes that his dignity is national, the result may be death but death in dignity.

Chance still remains for us Kenyans to transform the purpose of working from imprisonment in material value into freedom in moral value. While material value appeals to human lust and greed, moral value appeals to love and justice, i.e. the essence of common interests. When we study, farm and build things like hospitals, roads, schools and homes we achieve fulfilment in our lives which to attain is more important than the possession of these things themselves. A friend of mine was the other day very excited that he had organized the parents in his community school to construct two new classrooms and a swimming pool. This friend of mine, seems to have exchanged the value of having possessions to the value of uplifting his dignity through uplifting that of others. For this reason it is immoral for a young father and husband to abandon his family in order to go overseas for further education, leaving behind children without support and his wife without partner. Of course, education will increase the status, power and wealth but at high cost to human dignity. Here, at the level of the family, personal interests can be in conflict with common interests to the extent where this conflict affects the nation. To excuse negligence in the name of progress is tantamount to excusing our leaders too by carpets, expensive furniture for their offices and huge cars while farmers lacked diesel for their tractors and peasants lack paraffin for their kitchen.

Self-interests therefore when they become the main motivating force of political, economic and religious achievements lack the creative and visionary love that the family and the nation need in order to survive.

7.3 COMMON INTERESTS AS COMMON VALUE AND ACTIVITIES

When common interests manifest themselves in creative work like the sports, sportsmen feel dignified to play for their appreciative audience, regarding the audience satisfaction as the motivating force. Like sportsmen, preachers are motivated by the needs of the audience to speak out on important social issues. Human creativity aimed at mutual benefits produces in the process of work the feelings of self-worth, self-confidence and self-esteem whose value is greater than the final material product. A clerk who becomes obsessed in writing laws, circulars and directives for his clients and fails to enlist their co-operation finds himself frustrated and angry with his paper work. There is no dignity in associating a person with his products of work, such as appliances, clothes, papers, theories, dogmas and declarations while those meant to benefit from these feel alienated from him. Our interests in producing goods and services should go beyond the products themselves to the effects those products have on our relationships with the people using and affected by them.

If our investments and work has to do with the production of cigarettes and nuclear weapons we must have common interests with the people whose lives might be affected by nicotine and radiation. Human dignity has so much consciousness for collective responsibility that it does not allow one to produce knowledge, theories, plans, doctrines, drugs, poisons, vehicles, house, electronic devices, food or fabrics, without at the same time being concerned with the effects of the uses into which these will be put. Every producer is directly or indirectly responsible for the whole process of action, from production to the terminal use of the product however tiny is the part or role he takes in that process. If someone comes into your house with an axe seeking guidance of how to find your friend in order to kill him, failure to inform the police makes you an accomplice in the crime.

So our part in a process of action may be passive or active, but all the same we cannot be excused from the collective responsibility of what happens in our communities. I was once fined a thousand shillings for the failure of members of my family to chain my dogs, leaving them free to break the hedge and hurt a neighbour. Our laws which are aimed at protecting every citizen from unjustified injuries did not allow dogs to be responsible for themselves and therefore sought and found a person to blame for their actions. Similarly scientists and technicians cannot avoid responsibility for the use into which atomic energy might be put by war mongers. If we make weapons which others use to perpetrate crime against humanity we must speak out against such use like the Russian dissidents. Common interests require that we do not profit from causing misery to others. Dignity is pleased with itself when it is a master of none and slave to none, neither exploiting nor being exploited.

Dignity sees political independence, freedom, nationhood and development not only as products of past struggle but as a continuing process of action in which dignity continues to grow. Unfortunately, we have a generation of young people influenced by western culture who look at freedom and nationhood as static products not any different from cosmetics, ornaments, clothes, cars and refrigerators that deteriorate with age. To look at values of dignity, thus, liberty, justice, human rights and other results of political independence like toys is to value products more than the historical activities of human struggle that give meaning to human dignity. Some children especially those from privileged families play with out independence because they equate it with car models and dress fashions that they see their parents changing at will. They have failed to identify themselves with the actions of those who shed their blood to win that independence. They want to benefit from common interests while reserving themselves for selfish interests.

This perversion of values, exchanging moral values for material values is partly to blame on our educational system which lays emphasis on certificates instead of the whole process of learning and on religion which concentrates more on rewards in heaven than the ministry on earth. This makes people see everything in terms of its end rather than in terms of how the beginning, the means, the methods, actors and the end constitute a single whole. A society in which products are consumed without question as to their origin lacks conscience when human beings are enslaved, exploited and dehumanized under apartheid in South Africa to produce gold for enriching churches and markets in Christendom. Without identifying himself with the sick, lame, blind, hungry and imprisoned. Jesus Christ would never have been the Christ.

The true measure of dignity among people, or even whole societies, cultures and religions is in the moral quality of life they pursue in common and not in the material complexity, sophistication, wealth and power they pursue individually.

153

People may pile on themselves objects upon objects like Americans do, but the more objects they accumulate the less worth as human beings they are. The first time I came into conflict with American value of human beings as products was when I went to a missionary conference in Chicago where some "native Christians" from Asia, Africa and Latin America were displayed like cows in an agricultural parade. We were paraded like goods to show how missionaries had succeeded in producing civilized natives. In those circumstances I felt like a sheep among wolves and bears. Still worse than being treated like profits of missionary investments some of us behaved like first grade cattle ready to wear medals won by our benefactors. May be, they had to do that to get scholarships: The advantage of being black is that I was conscious of this as racism. Those of light colours from Asia and Latin America seemed to enjoy being displayed as the finnest products of the missionary enterprise.

Besides loyalty to my country the other reason I decided to return to the simple life in Kenya, after eight years of Babylonian captivity in America under white racism, was because I felt the danger of becoming spiritually bankrupt and morally alienated from my cultural background. My ability to acquire and accumulate material things heightened by self-interest so much that if I stayed there any longer, I risked losing touch with the common interests of my country. Material self-interests are still a poignant reminder to me that if I continue with westernization I may gain more worldly things and lose my spiritual identity. The choice became mine to abandon the values of the glistering gadgetry of chrome-plated cars, appliances, carpeted floors, cosmetics and cameras that appeal to self-interests or pursue them and lose the dignity of serving common interests. Ones culture and history are products of common interests that one cannot rub from his life in a day.

Finally, common interests derive from the dignity of people engaged in common political, religious, legal, social, cultural, educational, recreational or economic activities and who share common purposes and partake equally in losses and benefits. The history of common interests, just as much as of the common good, takes us back to the history of human dignity when men and women begun to harmonize their aims, reasons, purposes and conditions for existence with those of their neighbours. The critical transactions in their harmony was not in economic growth, though that was quite a necessary element of common interests, but in mutual care for one another. This makes the issue of development in Kenya today no longer the issue of increasing material goods alone but of the purpose for doing so. Our development has upto now laid too much emphasis on the western model of producing more and more goods, importing too much consumer, paraphanelia, and supporting private interests.

In this process, individuals have put morality aside in which the nation is in danger of being at the mercy of "survival for the fittest". The very people who put morality away when making profits by exploiting common interests, recover morality when they feel threatened by theft of the workers. This means that self-interests have no morality except when they want to attack the immorality of others in order for theirs to take root. All self-interest groups, whether military elites, politicians, priests, merchants or bankers like forgetting common interests when in control of the masses but remember them when challenged to surrender their privileges. However, nobody should pretend to be moral when morality means obedience to laws, commandments and restrictions that are imposed upon one faction of society by another. This leads us to conclude that our past struggle against alien domination by western colonial interests continues today as our struggle against internal factions of self-interests.

CHAPTER 8
HUMAN DIGNITY AND HUMAN ORDER

8:1 DIGNITY AND NATIONAL ORDER

Order is a regular pattern of predictable, rational and safe behaviour. It is the most effective system of human interaction and communication. We feel secure when our parents, friends, leaders and institutions do not keep on altering their behaviour, mothers are not likely to abandon their children and fathers honour their obligation to clothe and house them. God, nation or some other constant symbol of common identity is necessary for people to know that they are held together by one thing for common purpose. Unlike the mechanical order of the universe, human order is dynamic and delicate and is maintained by constant internal and external threat to it. National identity may be strong when faced with a common external enemy or when threatened by internal disintegration.

We have realized that human dignity and development are inseparable, since dignity requires institutions by which to serve, love and respect others. People cannot love one another in a group of over twenty million people, as in Kenya, unless this love is extended and communicated by their institutions, the state, church, school or hospital, of which the state is central. These institutions need harmony. It is human dignity that determines the harmony needed in these institutions to avoid being selfish, immoral and corrupt. A political, social, religious or economic institution is a medium of human dignity and always in danger of falling into sin and becoming a medium of vanity and evil. Even a legal marriage institution, sacred as it is, cannot communicate peace and love if the husband and wife lose their dignity.

People feel secure when sure that their family, customs and traditions follows certain regular procedures, laws, practices, customs and traditions when relating and communicating with them. They feel their rights violated when things are not done to them according to uniform procedure and practice. In order for people to invest their spiritual and material resources in any system of order it must be their own, not imposed. It must perpetuate their lives, self-discipline, love and unity. It must accommodate itself to their needs and problems, not its own demands. A good order is a reflection of the people's conscience. Human order is to human dignity what grammar is to language. A language will go to extinction unless it keeps on changing its rules to accommodate new ways of communication, regardless of how the rulers want their people to speak.

We have deliberately chosen the nation as the largest extent to which Kenyan families can become a family and feel themselves safe, the nation being as trustworthy and reliable as clans and tribes used to be in ancient times. We have heard of how other Africans in Nigeria and Uganda endangered their national order by allowing in it some relics of tribal power. Just as a family order can cause mental and economic disorder if it lacks human dignity, national order can cause all sorts of economic and social disorders if it allows conflicting and multiple identities to compete in it.

Kenya enjoys a code of ethics based on national identity to which all are expected to subscribe to, and that is, loyalty to the nation. This loyalty to the nation, with obedience to the state as the central system of authority does not exclude different and multiple expressions of loyalty through different religious, cultural, linguistic and economic systems. But there is only one political way of showing loyalty which proscribes and excludes all others, and that is the KANU party. But the country has proven safe, rational and predictable with many kinds of schools, religions, industries, languages and races. Capitalism in the guise of African socialism appears to be a part of this national order. No amount of corruption, bribery and sin has so far appeared to threaten our national order. But if this order were to interfere with the religions, customs, traditions, economies and institutions that tie people with it, people might lose hope in their ability to fight these crimes of corruption, bribery and sin and resort to chaos and anarchy. People may feel vulnerable when a school headmaster asks a mother of a student to bring fees during the evening at a

157

night club, but not resort to disorder if that mother has a central system where she can complain. Order needs checks and balances.

Nevertheless, rigid, inflexible, insensitive and authoritarian order, maintained by force for its own sake, can defeat the original purpose of maintaining and communicating dignity. Order is a "mass media", to transmit and communicate justice through various institutions. It cannot survive unless it keeps on re-ordering itself to accommodate new people, technology science and innovations. Order has the wisdom of many generations. It guarantees all people equal protection and opportunities and provides them with a peaceful environment conducive to development.

The religious and political order of Jesus' time had become destructive of human dignity by keeping rigid, unjust and inhuman customs, traditions and norms that divided people into separate caste, racial and class categories. The custom of separating men and women during public worship was strictly adhered to. Order was more important than human beings. The procedures, practices and customs by which this order was enforced were no longer based on human and godly justice but on the maintenance of order itself at all costs. The man was made for order and met order for man. Jesus' angrily protested against this corrupt order in which the Jewish leaders were against the sick being healed on Sabbath, and proclaimed "The Sabbath was made for man and not man for the Sabbath". Jesus directed that instead of order determining human dignity, it should be determined by it.

The most appropriate view of order, for Kenya and all other countries of the world, is, follow established laws, customs, practices, procedures, traditions, norms, theories and patterns that accommodate as many people as possible without disruption of order, as long as these enhance human dignity and incorporate new developments.

Human dignity is harmonious, peaceful and orderly. It creates an orderly environment. But the strength of order is tested by how much disorder it can allow to exist within it. Without elements of disorder in it, order will go to sleep. Order requires opposition, criticism and tests in order to be conscious of itself. Without temptations a person does not realize that he has an orderly approach to things, thus, conscience. If order fails to recognize dynamics within it and start fighting every challenge to it, it will disintegrate. While quite obedient to laid down procedures, customs, laws and expectations human dignity is not a slave to these but keeps on amending, renewing and transforming them to fit new situations.

Without this systemized behaviour in which individuals pursue personal benefits as a part of a whole community, love, peace, unity and just relations would be impossible. Without dignity as the basis of national order, the order outgrows its usefulness and sustains selfish interest by arbitrary means of coercion, force, exploitation, intimidation and disorder. People stop prolonging their lives and start fighting to kill or get killed. Instead of helping each other to solve natural problems they participate in the chaotic nd disorderly activities of alcoholism, crime, abortions, insurrections, riots and revolts. The moment respect and love of life, for its own sake, disappears everything orderly becomes disorderly. The politicians start telling the priests to keep off politics and the priests start to welcome politicians on the pulpit to defend the status quo. When order gives way to disorder, millions of people may get killed without anybody feeling any loss. Without order people act irrationally, each not being able to predict the actions of the other. It is indeed essential to national order that it has human dignity as the single criterion of measuring its own goodness, otherwise it becomes arbitrary and antithetical to the maintenance of human dignity. Only human dignity can maintain human dignity. When Jesus wanted to save mankind he gave his own life because only life could save life. The moment order becomes the tool of the state to protect itself from the people, people start fleeing away to seek refuge in other countries.

In other words, the Sabbath was made for man and not man for the Sabbath. The Sabbath lost its value the moment its laws required human beings to become its slaves and ceased to reflect the image of God that man was supposed to enjoy. Once man lost peace with God he became confused in his relationship with others and at war with himself. If the world loses peace with God and itself it automatically behaves violently against itself. This conflict and turmoil in the world comes from the evil of hatred.

"Love your neighbour" depends on loving them "as yourself". If one feels himself at the loose end of life, becomes uprooted from his job, suffers displacement from family and loses property because he is committed to love for others, he can suffer without bitterness and forgive those responsible for his persecution. But the moment a person suffers from selfish reasons he hates others and breathes brimstone and fire against them. In Kenya our harmony at the day of independence was the result of not sinning against those who had sinned against us. Those who had fought on the side of the British government to perpetuate colonialism were forgiven by President Kenyatta and regarded as if they too fought for independence. The greatest defeat Kenyatta would have suffered during his eight years of imprisonment would have been to alienate him from his people by making him hate some and fear others.

For this reason national order based on love, peace and unity is possible only when leaders are themselves in touch with the reality of national culture, history, hopes, economy, politics, dislikes, fears, goals, beliefs and aspirations. Our reality of social and national order in a small country like Kenya, with a small population compared to that of India or China can be easily managed not by being Indira Gandhi and Mao to Kenya but by allowing free and democratic expression of all those who wish to become leaders. The greatness of Kenya is not another great power but respect to its ways of doing things.

Dignity is an inclusive struggle for everybody to be what he can become and contribute his maximum for the orderly development of all. It is a ceaseless struggle to give honour to those we owe our civilization. We honour them by passing good aspects of African culture to the next generations. If we start fighting and quarrelling amongst us, our culture will be like that of Lebanon where struggle to give is unknown to those struggling against each other.

In traditional language, charity begins at home where a person is born and raised up to respect the socio-economic and political system of the family by which the community reproduces itself and projects its identity. In this sense national order begins in the family order where a group of people consisting of children, parents and relatives derive comfort, protection, education, and respect from one another. What happens in the family, the formation of common habits, customs, laws, infrastructures, values and co-operation under one common authority, projects itself in society as the national. order. The central national authority affirms the family authority and continues to care for and protect the family members, without replacing the family. It is only in the family where individuals can feel spiritual warmth and have peace, quietness, job, love, purity, continence, obedience, law, happiness and respect. The family is the foundation of national order upon which to construct national justice and freedom. It is a nuclear state, more committed to freedom, prosperity, and personal wellbeing than the larger nation state. The act of procreation and production of the next generations happens in the family as the point at which human order begins. The state cannot therefore justify its own existence if it does not regard families as its underlying systems of order. All systems in a nation whether the family institution or the government are held together by the common bond of human dignity.

The purpose of having a central authority is to unify and integrate various races, classes, tribes, clans, families and individuals into one nation, and in this process, to provide security, peace and justice to all people.

The central authority cannot achieve this objective without the consent and participation of those who are supposed to practise its laws and customs. If the state plays its own game with different rules of survival from the survival of the national population, then it ceases to be a legitimate part of the national order and becomes an element of disorder. The will to power should not be the sole key to remaining in power. Africa is tired of being an unruly and perfidious recipe for cooking *Coup' d'etats,* which has come a military picture of the day. Military, state or class order cannot be orderly unless it remains a component of the national order.

The key to the survival of dignity in national order is winning love and respect from the whole national population. Instead of eliciting fear by showing its force of uniformed soldiers, the state should respect people by providing them food, fertilizer, irrigation machineries and seeds for planting so that they can have independent means of survival. Hungry people do not anticipate bullets, teargas and helmets from their rulers but benevolence and sympathy. Sometimes the state is like a parent who takes care of children before taking care of himself. Dignity refuses being a slave of the work and choices of yesterday if they negate its freedom to procreate itself.

When Jesus Christ healed the sick and fed the hungry on Sabbath he demonstrated that God's kingdom puts human needs before its laws. God could not continue with the celebration of his own power on Sabbath while some people remained too sick, too weak and too hungry to participate in the celebration. One of the most brilliant action of the Kenya government in recent years was to parade trucks and trucks of yellow maize before the eyes of famine stricken members of Kenya population instead of parading military trucks full of silver bullets. This means that the Kenya government prefers life to death, respect to fear and dignity to tyranny. While other alternative methods of dealing with hungry people existed reason prevailed over them. Order was pursued with food rather than police.

Just as families preserve themselves in their children, states preserve themselves in their people. In other words a state perpetuates itself by perpetuating the dignity of its subjects. Some ignorant governments think of riots, insurrections, civil disobedience and rebellions as opposition governments trying to achieve them, and fail to see these as the suicidal actions of people desperately trying to use death as relief from their miseries. People prefer to die by the hands of their own government than exist without dignity. Otherwise people can endure extreme conditions of suffering, misery and torture trying to support their own government if they believe that its authority is a reflection and projection of that in their family. Even the most harmless, pious and delicate person will become violent against himself and others if cornered to believe that his life is useless and worthless before the eyes of his parents and government authority. A famous Kenyan psychiatrist told a group of prayer breakfast members that children who attempt suicide do so because dad or mum said a bad word to them which made them lose self-worth. Some of the social madness we see reflects mental chaos in the lives of individuals.

Dignity finds expression in orderly and organized structures. The family and the state are therefore the formal structures of human dignity. These external structures mirror the internal structures of how our minds are trained to operate. The state, as a projection of human desire for self-preservation can also be a projection of sinful desire for self-destruction if the men controlling it have suicidal tendencies which lead to war and violence. The lesser the legitimacy of the government the greater the use of force. The moment people cease to regulate themselves and need force to be under control they lose their orderliness, order and reason are two sides of the same coin. Use of force means the government having to attack or invade its own people militarily to enforce the payment of taxes or displacement of large numbers of people in order to protect and keep itself in order.

This means that while force is necessary for any government to keep order in society, under normal conditions, the government should rule by ethics consistent with the values and wishes of the people being governed. Most governments of the world, whether monarchies, aristocrasies, military, democracies, republics, empires, feudal, oligarchies, colonial, capitalist, socialist, federal, unions, agramain, industrial, western and eastern, and regardless of how they came into power, by heredity, elections, violence, revolution or colonization or *coup d'etat*, are agreed that force alone without the co-operation of those being governed, cannot sustain national order. When the human needs and problems of a national population exceed the capacity of the government to help resolve them peacefully the government will either encourage the people themselves to resolve them or resign. But it cannot delay solutions by use of force for ever. Any father, or leader, who uses a cane to discipline his child, or followers, does so only as a temporary measure to restore order, but once restored must be maintained by mutual collaboration.

It must also be emphasized that some of the institutions of society that the government licenses, such as businesses, industries, and religions would still continue to exist, even if they were not legalized. People will always produce things like food and clothes and will own something whether the state allows it or not. They will always worship their God and entertain certain beliefs with or without the law. The legality of such things is for orderly control and not for allowing or disallowing.

Governments, despite their monopoly of force and exclusive claim to power, belong to the same order of institutions as the churches, press, industries, markets, hospitals, universities, cultural centres, and trade unions. Their special role is like that of heads of families, to regulate the behaviour of children so that they do not injure one another. It regulates their lives by taxing, protecting and sometimes disciplining them. But regulation does not mean interfering with their internal constitutions and getting involved in how many bars of soap a shopkeeper can sell each day to avoid arrest, how many times a Muslim must pray per day to keep his job in the Mosque.

Hence a government that allows one class, group, institution, tribe, family or individual to dominate others or to advance its own interests at the expense of another renders itself ineffective and afraid of those that it alienates. There is nothing worse than power in the hands of a frightened government relying on military hardware than on people's loyalty and self-discipline. There is no purpose to have too many laws that one cannot enforce or make people to accept.

Some governments may feel themselves at the mercy of rich industrial or business corporations and allow them to exploit the workers and the poor. The governments power to administer justice and regulate these money-makers may be bought with huge contributions and bribes. This is why all social institutions, from the simplest one of marriage to the complex one of co-operative society must not be allowed to become richer and more powerful than the state. The economic power of the state must be greater than that of any other social institutions in order to avoid the situation where the government is unduly influenced by private interests.

Now comes the main question of checks and balances. If the government possesses the virtual monopoly of wealth and power, who checks its tendencies toward abuse and misuse? In cases of one party states which have not fears of ever losing power to another party the only way to check the abuse of power is regular election conducted on the basis of free and universal suffrage according to national constitutions. But for regular check up one organ within the body of the state such as the judiciary, parliament or administration can remind the other to account for its excesses. The judiciary can be the eye, the parliament the ear and the administration the hands of the same body.

But can a social institution like the University, the Industry, Commerce, Press or Church dare point at the problems plaguing the government at any time without being threatened with reprisals? What can the youth or intellectuals do to maintain their dignity of mind, free thinking and faith in a situation where their criticism might be taken as sedition against their regime? We must develop a culture of free exchange of opinions where central authorities get challenge to live according to their rules.

Nobody should contemplate, imagine or speculate of how to overthrow legally constituted authority unless it forces him to eliminate himself or accept elimination by others. Governments rise and fall with each succeeding generation, some lasting briefly and others for centuries depending on their support from the people or on the cohesion of the ruling class. But not so with the human spirit that constitutes the desire for order that lasts for ever. The human desire for order is not fixed to any specific institution though it may be attacked to the national governing authority that reflects its interests for a long time.

In the written history the Syrian, Assyrian, Babylonian, Persian, Greek, Roman and British empires maintained themselves for long periods because they subjugated people and colonized them without making them too resentful. They held the whip of oppression and exploitation in one hand and in the other the carrot of protection and rights to acquire personal property. In the eighteenth century, for instance, the weak countries in Europe sought the protection of the strong ones like France and Austria who exploited them. Wars by strong nations were fought on the territories of the weak ones. But today, it is the United Nations that assumes the role of a big empire from which small nations seek security. This security guarantees dignity. It used to be a mark of dignity for a small nation to submit to a bigger one for protection.

What has all this talk about the state and security to do with human dignity? The Bible, and indeed, the church history is full of incidences in which the state required to be worshipped. In some cases human beings had to be sacrificed by being forced to fight and kill each other to enterain the head of the state. Some kings amused their guests by having suspected criminals to fight with hungry lions barehanded. One of the funny enjoyment St. Augustine confessed as a great sin was to watch people being forced to fight one another for entertainment. Just as God who created the universe never washed his hands of it and still maintains moral and spiritual control in it, people cannot create states and wash their hands off how they behave. The people of Uganda never abdicated their rights to have moral influence over the actions of the state despite the cruel and brutal reactions by General Amin's State Research Bureau which martyred Archbishop Luwum. The fact that the church honours the state as the final and supreme authority in a given country does not mean that it must honour the crimes of those who pervert the state from being an instrument of order and justice.

As one who came to establish the kingdom of heaven on earth, of justice and orderliness in society, Jesus Christ declared for himself what the church claims to be its own faith, that "The spirit of the Lord is upon me because he has annointed me to preach good news to the poor. He has sent me to proclaim release to the captives and recovery of sight to the blind, to set at liberty those who are oppressed, to proclaim the acceptance year of the Lord." (Luke 4:18-19).

Jesus Christ believed that earthly powers are servants of the people in administering justice, healing the sick, helping the poor, feeding the hungry and freeing captives. Jesus projected this belief in his own personality by doing miracles to save rather than impress people. For this reason the instruments of power such as schools, hospitals, markets, churches, industries and armed forces are there to serve and not impress or exploit the people. Any army worth of its soldiers and country, and not in the interests of its own power. A humane army prefers to surrender and save the lives of its soldiers, if after thoughtful and careful evidence it calculates that the enemy has the capacity to destroy it at the ratio of a thousand to one without chances of escape. Just as armies are there to fight and win battles and not there to offer their soldiers as sacrifices to a blood thirsty enemy, all other institutions are there for the people and not the people for institutions. This means that the "Sabbath which was made for man" institutions fight battles for people and not people for battles. The human institutions must act on the basis of beliefs, principles, and hopes that their structures must deliver certain goods and services to the people and must never be maintained or defended to the extent where people offer goods and services to them.

The colonial rulers were not stupid. They have lacked compassion and justice but not knowledge and intelligence. Once they discovered that it was going to cost them more than they gained in their fight to suppress the Mau Mau freedom fighters they surrendered. While the British people may have had enough military power to rule Kenya longer than they did they surrendered to the Mau Mau desires for freedom because the emergency had made the cost of ruling Kenya higher than economic and political benefits. The British people were in Africa not to help Africans maintain law and order but to use law and order as instruments of capitalist profits. From the point of view of common sense the British empire could not continue killing people for the sake of killing them while the original purpose of economic profits was defeated by their revolt.

Having already argued that while the state has a monopoly of power and force it has no monopoly of everything in a country, how can it ensure that various social institutions do not create conditions for civil conflicts, rivalry and frictions? Of course, a church may have monopoly over its own doctrines and sacraments but not to the extent of using force to impose them on others. But in situations like Sudan it is the government which favours the Muslim sect against the Christian and Traditional religions. In some other countries the state may appear to be under the influence of one race against another as in South Africa. There was a time when Liberia used to be controlled by large American corporations which controlled rubber plantations before the days of synthetic rubber. In some national institutions in, Kenya it might appear that there is one tribe more predominantly in control than others. This is dangerous to social and orderly justice.

Some conflicts are a necessary evil between private institutions that have no political power, for intance between drugs' manufacturers and doctors, churches and breweries, and status quo and arnachists. An orderly system which cannot allow conflicts between workers and employees, and tenants and landlords leaves some people exposed to abuse and exploitation by others. Some contradictions in every system are very necessary for its healthy function. Willing buyers and willing sellers must collaborate with each other in a healthy trade function without allowing their conflicting interests to disrupt trade which is their common interest. While their claim is to take as much from one another their rules of conflict are the necessary contradictions of maintaining negotiation, bargaining and agreements toward better existence.

The problem comes when in this competitive collaborations in conflict the brewery companies give huge donations to church projects to bribe pastors against criticism of drunkness. Some churches borrow tents with brewery signs to advertise alcoholic drinks while at the same time organizing projects to deal with drug addictions. Robberies, negations and crimes may be introduced by some parties in a conflict but this reflect disorder and social sickness rather than health competition.

In a healthy conflict churches can point at cerain malfunctions, mistakes, problems and abuses in the system without having to interfere with the internal mechanisms of how it operates. Similarly the government can legislate laws to control all social institutions including the church without interfering with the internal mechanisms of running the church like church doctrines, government, beliefs and leadership.

In this sense the church can retain its nature as a sign of God's kingdom with its own internal structures and rules without being rival and negative to the national state. Many parallel forces, organizations and institutions can exist in one nation as long as one of them, the state, has a monopoly of force and retains legislative authority over the others. In this sense, a Christian is a child and citizen of two kingdoms, one of the world and the other of heaven. As a citizen of the world he must obey all government laws which do not require that he violate the commandments of loving God and loving his neighbour as himself. If the state requires that a Kikuyu should take an oath "tea" of hatred against a Luo or any other human being belonging to another tribe or race, the Christian may chose to disobey and if possible resist the sinful oath. The heavenly kingdom is of grace and love toward all people and of peace and goodwill toward the whole world. A ruler who loses his theological legitimacy to rule may rely only on his military and police force to maintain himself in power but loses support from the affections, love, and conscience of the people.

God's kingdom of peace, justice and love by which our earthly kingdoms must pattern their behaviour is concerned with the plight of every man's existence and accommodates to all the institutions that help man to enjoy life whether these are aware of God's kingdom or not. God does not care with whom he shares power as long as the power is shared to administer justice.

When God humbled himself in the incarnation of Christ Jesus he became the model of how Christians must condescend and work within the frameworks of existing national laws. But Christians must always remain conscious of themselves as children of God, helping God to create governments and laws that conform to God's will. And since all public institutions are made by man for man, and never man for them, man must remain free of them not their slave. President Kenyatta used to repeat this very often in his speechs, that the ordinary person is the master of the government, not the government his master. Jesus Christ whipped and chased out of the temple those who exhorted the temple above the people, and the extent of using the temple as a means of exploiting and exorting money from the people. While people are servants of the law, this being servants makes them masters at the same time, not slaves. They organize governments, churches, clubs and unions in order to perfect their service to each other and make that service effective and efficient and must never sacrifice this purpose to law and order for their own sake. Law and order are instruments of achieving peace, justice and service but not masters. For this reason, it means that any national order, whether political or economic exists solely for the purpose of maintaining human dignity. National order is therefore the maintenance of human dignity in a social context in which everybody shares the same obligations, rules and goals. Without uniform law covering everybody in the same national system there would be chaos.

8:2 THE MAINTENANCE OF ORDER BY INTELLECTUAL RESOURCES

So far, we have seen that national order is there for human dignity and not human dignity for national order. Many authors of religious political, sociological and economic text books have different definations of national order that validate the point Jesus Christ made that "the Sabbath was made for man and not man for the Sabbath". Intellect is also a talent or gift from God for use to serve others and not for sale. Intellectuals should benefit from their mental work from the benefits others receive from that work but not directly.

But without the Sabbath, thus, good medical, educational, water, economic and political system, man cannot survive in peace. While man does not exist to eat, without eating, he would die. The choice is not whether we eat or not, whether we have order or not, but what kind of food or order we want to have. The rules of getting what we want are in an orderly system called equal opportunities for all and rewards based on merits. The quality of our choice is determined by human intellect.

In a text book entitled *"Development Administration"* according to *"The Kenya Experience"* I noticed that our political administration is very conscious of its responsibility for using intellectual resources as instruments of creative, innovative and new developmental activities, instead of continuing to use law and order as repressive and oppressive instruments of power. Whether our political administration has succeeded in this transformation of law and order into intellectual tools of fighting ignorance, disease, sickness and inequalities is not our major concern at the time being. Our main interest is how human dignity, at all levels of social institutions, even in the civil service, can be the criterion of measuring whether human beings are benefiting from national order or are being used as mere objects of perpetuating national order.

Education itself can become a form of national intellectual order to which the country sacrifices a lot of material, personnel and children without bringing any benefits to them or the country. The African intelligensia, the most self-righteous of all power groups in the country, believes that learning a lot of things qualifies them for better pay whether they produce the goods or not. It analyses problems of poverty, injustice and inequalities in society, makes conclusions about how these can be abolished, presents these to seminars and examiners, but does nothing beyond intellectualism. This means that education, as part of our national order may have no other practical value than examination papers, articles and official reports. This would mean that education has failed completely to produce men and women who know the right behaviour, are self-disciplined and have intellectual skills to solve any problem confronting them personally and socially. The main benefits of education is not that people will earn better wages but that they will be more orderly, having learned all the rules, customs, traditions, history and abilities of their country.

Despite its size in numbers the Kenya intelligensia does not conduct its administration, farming, industries and churches better than those who barely know how to read and write, and feels lost when not in classrooms elaborating it's theories before the other intelligensia. Academic order, as an exercise that consumes a disproportionately bigger part of our national budget than other services does not offer solutions to most of the problems that exists in society but only compounds them by being a heavy economic burden. The purpose of our universities and colleges is not to produce intellectuals but intelligent answers to our problems.

Any form of national order which creates its own ethics, which if examined in the light of others, ends up being an isolated and negative within order, must be changed to conform to the rest of national order. Whether it is a teacher, evangelist, chief, lawyer or engineer working for certain institution within our national order, he should recognize his role as contribution to the integrity of the whole order, and not as an independent entity. Intellectualism is not a special order but a small part of the national order system. It should pay social dividends.

The reason our intelligensia becomes parasitical rather than creators, innovators and organizers of new solutions to human problems is lack of intellectual dignity. Their education from kindergarten to university gives them arrogance rather than confidence, pride rather than self-esteem, self-concept rather than self-respect. Of course they have some dignity which does not match their academic knowledge. In other words they lack wisdom. They therefore regard themselves as a superior sub-order within national order. They imagine themselves of being managing directors of big companies, parliamentarians and bishops so that they can allocate themselves huge salaries and allowances, according to their "intelligence". They would do this being thoroughly knowledgeable and having written in examination papers that their country suffers from unemployment, shortage of investments, poverty and sickness and requires the tightening of belts. They are more self-conscious as a group, elite or class than belonging to the nation.

National order, in order to be truly national must regulate all other forms of order within it by following a common code of conduct in which all forms of development are focussed into one. Dignity is an educated person being conscious of his debt to the nation that spend resources on his education expecting benefits.

This would make the people of knowledge, as much as of power and wealth, realize that before using the national order for their own benefit, this being the very reason it exists, should offer their own lives to create those benefits. The benefit of their work should come to them indirectly having already benefited everyone.

Once people realize that the national order, thus, the Sabbath does not exist without them and is their own creation, they will give their intellectual service to it. In other words, we take care of the institutions that take care of us. Any institution that we exploit misses human dignity and in turn starts to exploit us. If driven by the ethic of overtaking the masses and workers in order to pay educated people for their education regardless of the relevance of that education then we have created a Sabbath that exploits us. This is the situation in which Jesus Christ found the people in relation to the Sabbath, the Sabbath being used by the Rabbis, Pharisees and law makers as a means of exploiting and oppressing the people, without any regard to its original meaning of peace and rest. We educated people must give our dignity to our national order so that it has dignity to give us. What we sow in these national institutions is what we reap. Whatever we expect from our country we must give it to it first. Intelligence is a raw resource that we must give to our country like we give hay to a cow to produce milk for the people.

Since national order is a projection of who we are, our works, attitudes, thoughts and actions, it cannot have the dignity which we have not given it. We should expect rational laws, reason and justice from our national institutions because these are the things we have invested in them. Just as you cannot expect your bank account to have the money that you have not yourself banked, you do not expect that a public institution will have the logic, justice and affection that the workers in that institution have not put into it. Dignity is the law from which all laws are derived. It is a law consistent with itself because it starts with people themselves, becomes national and then comes back to the people.

It is human beings who invest their dignity in the national order in order for it to yield dignity. The minds and actions of the rulers and leaders of a country are trained by their work to correct what goes wrong without recourse to force. The mental abilities of rulers become the mind of the state, and their actions the actions of the government. If they have a corrupt irrational mind which assumes that poverty, sickness and ignorance are due to laziness and genetic inferiority, they will tend to strengthen the army and the policy to deal with social problems but if they have a pure and holy mind which assumes that even the sick, poor and ignorant are the children of God, they will tend to strengthen the welfare and development programmes. Although our constitution stresses that every person is "entitled to the fundamental rights and freedom of the individual whatever his race, colour, creed or sex", without a human mind correspondent to these constitutional guarantees some people will never know that a good national constitution guarantees them dignity. Some people may exist in a society which denies them access to essential services, especially education, health, security and markets and never know that they are being denied such things. All they do is blame themselves for their misery and wish they were born rich, educated or healthy. They take their misery as a curse from God. Such fatalistic approach to life becomes their lack of dignity in the national institutions which fail to enlist the masses in their own development. It is this fatalistic resignation, docility and submission to inequality and in justice that some leaders think of as order. Before God this apparent order was moral disorder.

Dignity for all people should be the criterion of i ...nitiating local projects for self-development to redress economic imbalance between social classes. The way to stop government neglecting their constitutional role of initiating development is not to overthrow them as often happens in Africa but to have governments whose closeness to the people would make them impossible to challenge.

This means that a government governs by correcting inequalities, imbalances and other seeds of disorder by fair distribution of services and means of survival. Every human being desires attention by the national institutions, whether the church or state and must have a share of medical, educational and food resources, no matter where he is, in prison or in the village. Even a criminal condemned to life imprisonment requires his mind to recieve education and his soul to receive spiritual comfort. History tells us that any society cannot be orderly to the point of having no criminals, patients, invalids, mentally insane and imbeciles in its national order to take care of. It is unfortunate that we have abandoned the idea of forced labour in our system of economic justice. This is because forced labour started in 1919 to force Kenyans to work for colonial settlers and later became abolished to avoid insurrections. But if the people were being forced to work for themselves and this being limited to two years in work settlements, by the end of two years people would never wish to stop working. Mwea Irrigation Scheme is a case in point where Mau Mau detainees preferred to stay behind working as rice growers even after having been released. Education aimed at the benefit of children and work aimed at the self-reliance of the unemployed should be enforced without moral problems.

A national youth service, compulsory for all school leavers who cannot be immediately absorbed into the paid employment sector is essential to avoid unemployment which humanizes people by boredom, idleness and disillusionment. Forcing somebody to take medicine for his own health is not the same as forcing him to lose something.

175

Power does not always equal the amount of force the government is capable of using to protect itself from the people but can be diversified to protect the people from natural enemies like diseases, economic enemies like famine, and social enemies like alcoholism and crime. It is better to see a government using force to have people vaccinated and immunized against cholera, T.B., polio and D.P.T. for children, than to use military tanks, rockets, missiles, guns and troops to protect them from an imaginery foreign enemy. To see human dignity in the state and institutional machineries of national order is more important than to see statistical figures of how much the state spends on military hardware. In other words, a strong government is secure because the population has confidence in it and see their own dignity in its services but not because of its capacity to yield violent force. Violent force may be used in certain conditions under limited circumstances such as dealing with armed bandits but must never be used as an answer to food, employment, labour, and developmental issues. These issues need planning, reasoning, investments and reformation to resolve.

The problem with most African governments is the failure to distinguish between people demonstrating for milk, water and grains and demonstrating for power. If the powers that be feel that they do not wish people to have water and other means of existence, then they may use any possible means to suppress the demonstrators. Many despotical and tyrannical rulers have throughout human history destroyed their kingdoms by cruel use of force by the state because it fears the people put more fear in the people than the state can control, thus leading to all sorts of refugee, rebel and banditry problems. Trust and not fear is the best covenant between people and their governors. While trust is an expression of dignity, fear spells antagonisms and tends to invalidate free and lawful relationships. The democratization of any system is tested its success by how it resolves problems, in orderly manner. It is by studying the problems around us, not proclamation and directives, that produce the solution.

8.3 DIGNITY AS THE RIGHT USE OF POWER AND SELF-DEFENCE:

Power is the ability to make things happen or to stop them from happening. One can compel others to act by promising them money or by threatening to curse them, or can stop others from acting by standing on their way or by disagreeing with them. A mother may stop her children from fighting by feeling angry and may cause them to work hard by feeling happy. The best form of power is when people can do what you want to avoid upsetting you or to please you. This is the power of mutual friendship, treaties, agreements, covenants, constitutions, fraternities, fellowship and love. Power has dignity when it achieves its end without using tricks, threats or force.

There is power to reward or deprive someone according to his behaviour. This is similar to the power of approval or disapproval. The greatest power over me is the approval or disapproval by God, thus, the power of scripture, creeds, confessions and church over my life. This power is never physical but spiritual. I can be threatened with death because of my loyalty to God and yield nothing but I cannot bear to live if God would refuse to forgive my sins and turn away his love from me. There is dignity in my life only in relationship to God's power. I believe that he uses it for my salvation. This saving power of God can be found in governments, companies, families and leaders in different ways.

While no man should be obliged by law, torture or threat to accuse himself without assurance of pardon, in some countries suspected criminals are subjected to harassment to incriminate themselves by signing police statements written against them. A wife, father or guardian is supposed to represent God in his relationship with the husband and child and should never aid accusors, in a civil state or others in punishing them. The testimony of a wife against a husband or child against a father is the wrong use of power and is a sign of corruption in human morality. Therefore, a person should never use force against himself or his family even if forced to do so by the state. However if tortured by the state, or police to accuse oneself or ones family, and one yields due to pain, in the case of those who have to yield to avoid getting killed in the process of torture, after surviving the torture and having escaped to safety one can be excused for his mistake, after repentance. He can claim that the right to preserve his life prevailed over the right to preserve his dignity. But in cases where one is sure that he will get killed whether he confesses against himself or not, then he must accept to die in dignity and not confess. A pastor would also prefer to suffer to death than disclose secrets confessed to him by his church members.

A human being should never agree to get killed or kill himself. Similarly he should never consent not to defend himself from external forces if attacked. The Court of Kenya, under our constitution does not allow anybody to forfeit his right to defend himself even from the state when threatened by death, imprisonment or fine. According to law one is able to hire lawyers to defend him and call witnesses to support his defence. In other words, the constitution follows the Old Testament books of Exodus, Leviticus and prophets where man owes his life to God alone and has no right to give it to anyone or anything for any reason. When threatened by death it is better to die resisting it than yield to it. Only a person likely to defend himself to the last chance can be entrusted with the lives of others. National oaths and church vows are null and void if the person swearing holds his life cheaper than he can die defending. Only those who can defend themselves can defend others. Christ died fighting against evil forces and never quit fighting to defend the kingdom of God, and he in a spiritual manner keeps on fighting, getting wounded and dying for us, as members of his family. His right use of power was not to kill his enemies but to resist their power to the point of death. The living body of a person is the least unit of life by which dignity exists and the family the least institution by which dignity is preserved. Just as a person must die defending his body and family, he must also die for the nation because it is an extension of these.

Supposing the university students want to stage a demonstration against the will of the state. The government aware that the university is one of the systems and institutions of its own order, and by use of authorities in the university may use its power by suspending students or closing the university, or may use physical force by arresting them and charging them with disturbance of peace, or may, choose to use excessive force by shooting them. Normally, what happens is that the students are sent home to their parents and their graduation is affected. Once the students are back to school they may regroup and become even more highly organized to stage another demonstration than before. Students politics therefore becomes integral part of the national order in which power to enforce law and order becomes the official response. Only that this power is applied as suspension of students benefits and not for the malicious purpose of violent destruction. Any use of power to enforce law and order and from a legitimate source should not resort to violence. Violence may be used only as the last resort when the body of the nation or national integrity is threatened like a man must defend his own body if threatened.

Violence is the misuse and abuse of power to force someone act against his own wish. It is also the use of excessive, uncontrollable and unjustified force to achieve aims that would have been achieved by means of persuasion, negotiation, and reconciliation. It is violent to use force illegally, illegitimately and maliciously to cause disorder, death, inconvenience, imprisonment, enslavement, oppression, exploitation, suppression, maiming and suffering of an innocent person. But if the person, group, organization or mob against which violence is used by the state initiated its use by resisting arrest in a violent manner, enough violence to disarm and subdue them must be used.

Violence can be any threat to use force or actual use of force to deprive an opponent his life, property, means of existence, freedom, shelter, opportunities for relief, access to medicine and food, escape from danger and friendship. While violence is normally committed by means of bombs, guns, spear, gases, fire, poisons, vehicle, fists and chemicals it can be equally destructive to use social, economic and psychological means. Once an opponent is conquered by physical means subjection can be enforced by deprivation of food, medicine, education, association and essential services. This can also lead to psychological warfare where the victim is segregated, discriminated, ridiculed, disregarded, neglected, overtaxed, hated, abused, laughed at and ashamed. The use of any of these methods to maintain order proves the existence of disorder. It is national sickness to maintain internal disorder by external force. People may obey out of fear but not out of love.

Some of the ways violence is used against someone may be so subtle and hidden that it destroys personality leading a person to die of sorrow, alcoholism, self-pity and suicide. One can die due to violence without knowing and without blaming those who destroyed his dignity. But it makes no difference whether he died for lack of self-respect, essential commodities or died for burning, bombing or poisoning. The fact is that both methods can injure, inflict pain and kill. The best order is the one in which people rule themselves by their own rules, leaders and system.

The third category where power can be used to enforce certain behaviour or to discourage another is by temporary withdrawal of rights or priviliges such as expelling striking students from school, taking condemned man to prison for a definite period. Retiring somebody or dismissing him from employment when he fails to perform his duties, denouncing certain behaviour in the press to put stigma in somebody's reputation if that person sells drugs without valid permit, discriminating against certain classes, groups or persons which in many cases can lead to civil war, holding somebody to ridicule, fining or confiscating goods, demoting someone, ostricising one from the system or transfering a person from one place to another.

All these uses of power are good if used for constructive purposes like stopping immorality, wickedness, crime, rebellion or violence to continue but evil if all they do is to add injuries. But force, except for self-defence must never be used by someone who tempts rather than discourages his opponent to use it. A father can spank his son of one to twelve years with his cane on the buttocks but cannot do the same with a son of twenty one years without provoking him to fight. Any use of power that provokes insurgency, riots, insurrections, rebellion or violence portrays the weakness of the user. The moment a governing authority resorts to violence to deal with violence or to lawlessness to deal with lawlessness it appears to recognize the existence of other states or governments within the same nation. It alienates the community, or at least some members of the community and compels them to join these other counter-violent forces. The government should always be in complete control of power, its own and that of any other institution whether a bank, company, trade union or church and must never allow itself to be in competition with them. government which reacts to lawlessness by lawlessness or chaos by chaos drives those within it, be they soldiers or civilians to lose confidence in national security. Let the government appear to defend someone under its care when it uses force or violence but never appear to defend itself. Let it appear to intervene to save someone from danger.

When a government can close markets, schools or factories to effect its control and keep law and order, or collectivize the people into villages to contain their activities and monitor their movement, then it is in power. Supposing a village chief wished to send all the villagers away the way he sees the university authorities doing to suppress students' demonstration. This would be an act of violence against citizens beyond bearable amounts. The reaction of the people may not lead to immediate insurrection or violent conflicts but will leave the chief without people to rule. To dismantle villages, towns and cities is not as easy as dealing with a school strike by sending children to their homes. Power should always be used on the side of the people and on their behalf, otherwise it loses its legitimacy. A father applies pressure or canes the child for the child's benefit but not for his own pleasure as the father.

The best and most effective use of power is to command respect and provide security besides helping people in improving their conditions of existence. The best use of force is never to allow a situation which requires its use. And if it has to be used never use it to tempt your opponents to use it, but always try to disarm and discourage them from using it, otherwise your cost of using it may be too high and so prolonged that you will regret. The best order is a natural one where people live together in harmony without any need for violent intervention. Natural order resolves its problems politically, religiously, medically, commercially and legally without resulting to disruption.

The best way to use force is never to use it. Prepare for war and expect none. But if it is necessary to use force never use it beyond stopping others from using it. Beyond the use of force to restrain force, force becomes mere violence and disorder. Force is a necessary element of national order and no national order can exist without it but beyond the maintenance of order it has no other function. Only the government has no right to dismiss his worker without government consent, which means without due and lawful reasons of doing so. Similarly a headmaster should not discipline a student unless he acts on behalf of the government, that is, within the law. Even a church or any other religious organization acts on behalf of the state when it uses any form of power to punish, dismiss or rebuke its members and would be committing a crime against the national order if it deprived a church employee his wages without legal justification. Of course, markets, industries, churches, firms, clubs and social institutions do have their own regulations and semi-autonomous laws, but these remain part and parcel of the national systems.

In fact, there is no place in the world for absolute power by any social organization, be it the state or army. Within the state itself, among its employees, executive and decision makers there are dynamics of power in which power is shared by various organs to stop its concentration on any individuals. In Kenya power is not only shared between various ministries in the government but the government itself has three main systems of power, the judiciary, the legislature and the executive. It is also delegated from top to bottom in such a way that a village chief may have some powers which the Provincial Commissioner does not have. The Chiefs Act is a case in point. The more decentralized and diffuse the power, the more pervasive and the better its influence. Even in the human body all power is not concentrated in the head, some is in the heart, liver, kidneys, feet and reproductive organs.

Influence and not force should be the best way to use power. We clergy are powerful people in our society. Yet we have no way of converting our power into force. Our power is always in the form of influence and can sometimes influence other powers to use force without implicating ourselves. A single priest can influence a community to build schools, hospitals, roads, industries and markets where none used to exist and be more effective than a civil administrator taxing and forcing the community to do the same. My influence as a husband and father in my family achieves better results than my capacity to use force. Influence is mutual power where you allow yourself to be influenced by those you influence.

Finally the right use of power depends on the attitudes of the population. All power is based on and in fact requires consent to use it. You can command an army to shoot, but not shoot. An army general may command his soldiers to bomb a church where the families of his soldiers go to worship or an emperor direct his admirals to destroy a camp where their families are held hostage but with no effect. Power is therefore not a closed system without custom, beliefs, affections, emotions and second thoughts. A Christian army will disobey commands to bomb a children's hospital because of the godly influence in it. Power is an instrument of order. Every order produces power. You cannot have order and not have power. The energy human beings produce with their minds when together is power. The power can be bad or good. The kitchen knives mothers use for cutting potatoes for their children can cut children instead of potatoes if mothers were to cease being mothers and became armies of invasion against their children. In every human being there are unconscious processes tending toward use of power for peaceful ends but which if threatened tend toward violence. So, let us not threaten our governments in case they are tempted to use force. Power is good when used for peaceful ends.

But we are now sure that though political power requires the monopoly of force, force alone is an inadequate basis of ability to govern. Cultural values in which people have

183

favourable attitude toward their rulers especially toward the president of the country are of critical importance in the maintenance of national order. The right use of power is to influence, not to force except where influence has exhausted its effects. Only when power yields to its own inner temptations to enforce its own desires whether right or wrong does it lose its moral influence, "tends to corrupt and corrupts absolutely".

8.4 ORDERS AS A MEANS TO SECURE BETTER EXISTENCE

Human dignity requires a social existence with respect to human life. The right to secure means of existence is a part of orderly community. But being orderly alone is not enough given that a plantation where a master owns a thousand slaves or exploits a thousand labourers can appear orderly while people continue to die due to lack of proper health facilities, schools and food. Order can exist for evil daily by hundreds due to cholera, industrial accidents and pollution. Justice is an essential element of good order. God called men like Moses to liberate his people, his people from Egypt where order was there to facilitate oppression, exploitation and slavery and helped him free them toward better existence.

Order is a perfect way in which things are placed in relation to one another like the alphabet or the planets so as to be able to predict their behaviour in their relationship to one another. One can arrange slaves and masters, colonized and colonizers, poor and rich, men and women and powerful and powerless in a perfect order in which some allow others to suck their blood. If a certain order is such that the whites take advantage of blacks, then the order is contrary to God's will and must be regarded as disorder in God's kingdom. While order is difficult without peace there should be no peace without justice. Order is there to represent the beliefs, preferences, perceptions, needs, purposes, plans, policies and opinions of the people and must assist them in their struggle for development. The dignity of a country like Kenya consists of its ability to help its people feed themselves, clothe and house themselves and educate their children. It must also provide health facilities and police security to enable them work without physical or social constraints. There is no dignity in poverty except if one is poor for charitable purpose.

Order is therefore a dynamic interplay of various forces that exist together in one country held together by a more powerful and superior force called the state. There is no national order without national unity based on a certain physical, historical, social, cultural, religious, economic and political reality consisting of people and their possessions. The most valuable of these possessions is the people's geographical location measured in square kilometres and whose every milimetre must be defended by life. Territory is a supreme value for nationhood because life depends on its space. It is the right to occupy space which preceeds right to live. Where we were born is important as when we were born. God's promises to Abraham included first land and secondly posterity. Before God blessed Abraham to become a father of a great nation he promised him a certain space in the universe. In fact, the earth was created before man. Before man was created all the physical assets, earth light, water, vegetable and animals were already created so that he can have the means of existence. I always say that I can offer my life for three things, my country, my church, and my family. In my country are included my president, anybody lawfully staying in Kenya, and the territory with all its contents. The ethnic forces that belonged to Luo Union, GEMA, Akamba Association and others were disbanded by President Moi to eliminate seeds of social and national disunity. Kenya is our common resource and nobody has more right to enjoy it than another.

Where multiple identities exist in one country as in Nigeria and Uganda the country can suffer a lot of violence based on tribal animosities. In Kenya there may be a few Asian or European activities based on their clannish, racial or cultural backgrounds, and when it comes to wholesale business and industries causing jealousy among Africans, but these do not constitute a threat to national unity. If the Kikuyu or Luo were to behave like Patels in their businesses, when it comes to the allocation and access to resources such as business, education and medicine, the happiness of the whole population is more important than of any tribe, race or class.

This means that national order consists of national dignity for all in concrete and tangible forms in the fair and just sharing, distribution and allocation of resources. In practical terms a civil servant entrusted with the management of a state hospital should never have a private clinic of his own and a Provincial Commission should not belong to a clan or tribal association. The smuggling of essential goods and handling of important commodities like food and medicine in Kenya happens because of private and sectional interests. You can see Africans queuing for rice, flour and sugar during shortages and never see any other race in similar predicaments. I noticed, during a petrol shortage that only Africans and visitors lacked petrol and had to drive all the way to Karen in a European neighbourhood to have my car filled, between 1980 and 1982. This means that certain private economic sectors of our society, operating legally under Kenya law do not co-operate with the government in its aim to serve all people equitably but they put self-interests above national interests. This is a threat to common interest and national identity.

Any private or sectional interests that conflict with national ones become a threat to national order and peace. Since the life of every member of the population depends on security on others, on those working in the armed forces, civil service or in essential services, those entrusted with such security should never be allowed to have alternative sources of security for themselves. National leaders should therefore never be allowed to have monetary accounts in banks outside their own country or any allegiance to institutions in foreign countries. Nobody should have security outside the institutions that provide security to his fellow citizens. Even the president of a country should rely for his security on the same national wealth, resources, armed forces, concerts and hospitals on which every other citizen depends. Any source of security for one citizen which is not available to all makes some citizens insecure.

There should be no distinction between the security of the

people and of the government. The city soldiers should not burn the shanties of the poor people unless they have alternative homes for them. Squatters must be protected from harassment by landlords in the same way landlords are protected from harassment by land grabbers and if necessary new settlement areas where squatters can own plots be found. In our national order system, all are equal.

In order for people to feel secure and safe in their country, the state must ensure that their rights to self-preservation are reinforced by the police. The police must be available to answer their calls and reports and to provide them means of escape from any danger. A dignified state is the one in which the police can protect mentally disturbed people from harassment by the public and rescue families from a depressed maniac. The police uniform must be associated with love for the insane, criminal and abnormal. The human way it protects them in its action of arresting and confining them demonstrates that national resources are benefiting everybody. God, in Jesus Christ, offered possibilities that power means ability to rehabilitate sinners and sick and not to destroy their personalities more than sin has already done. In this sense better existence may not only be good for the corporate rich, educated elite and power possesses but for the outcasts, marginals and poor.

National betterment must therefore enhance the national efforts to make existence secure for all people, even the mentally handicapped, cripples, outlaws and criminals. A criminal must be protected from mob justice and instant executions without trial. A dignified nation demonstrates its dignity not only through military parades and wavings of flags but in minimizing the use of force and minimizing programmes to reduce crime, violence, suffering, hunger, injustice and despondency.

National order is therefore an instrument of power which helps people if in the hands of dignified rulers. The individuals who offer to serve others through the machinery of national power should regard themselves as agents of God's justice which provides security for all. They have the love that denies itself for the sake of others.

National order expresses itself in concrete and practical programmes of helping the poor. Offering food to children that belong to a poor family is the work of the national order to which these children are born. Any person acting as a unionist, commissioner, priest, social workers, or businessman is a father and a mother to all children in his community regardless of whether these are his own or belong to another. This is what distinguishes national order as human concern from national order as an institution of domination.

In a human and legitimate order there is nobody, however old or young, healthy or sick or intelligent or mentally slow not accounted for. All human relationship are governed by the same order and recognized as important to human dignity. For instance, a marital relationship is given legal sanction or public recognitions so that the boys or girls who wish to be husband and wife can be protected from others. Lovers can become the most enemies, steal from one another and neglect each other if their love has no moral, social and legal sanction other than romance. Lovers can form the best orderly relationship as long as they remain in love most of or all their lives. But some last longer than their partners who need legal guarantees that what they possess together belongs to each one of them equally when both are alive and wholly when one of them dies. Even when one partner dies before the other, the history, property, body, grave and losses remain the resources of the other.

This brings us to the question of men-women relationship in the national order. Both men and women have equal relationships in access to opportunities, promotions, sex, status, position, leadership and ownership. None receives favour from the other, all are equal in their rights to fair competition, meritorious gains, reward and punishment.

In my family background there was a sense in which all people regardless of sex or status are equal. The question of favour does not arise. My family (clan) acts like a government full of welfare and social services extended to all equally whether they reciprocate or not. If a rich member of the family slaughters a goat to celebrate Christmas, a new born baby, the return of a person from several years of absence, or a wedding, every member of the family with his or her friends are invited. The poor cousins. nephews, widows. orphans and children call each other and bring their friends to come and enjoy the feast. They come in such great numbers because this gives them self-respect, self-confidence and dignity. When they are many they can eat, drink and dance without feeling that they owe anything to anybody. There are happy that a member of their family can afford to slaughter a goat for them but would be unhappy to think that the goat was slaughtered to show off or to slight anybody. Nobody wants the debt of feeling that he or she owes the piece of meat he or she eats to the rich man. It belongs to them as a family. It would humiliate and indignify a poor member of the family to imagine that he would be asked to pay for the joy to socialize with others by sharing a meal with them.

This kind of primordial structure of family order in which a family meal makes existence better for all should be the model of national order. The country must have a state which behaves like a rich member of the family who slaughters a goat for all to feast but expects no thanks, reciprocation or fees. This is why education, medicine, transport, housing and school uniform should be provided free to all citizens by the state. The state is the greatest form of extended family and should possess, organize and run all the essential services in the country. It should according to the means of existence to all equally and unconditionally. The equality, justice, freedom and peace of every child and adult in a country is the business of the state. Whether one is a naturalized citizen or a citizen by descent or birth he or she is a member of the national family with equal claims and rights to national means of existence.

However, individuals do have freedom of privacy, ownership, speech, association, worship, movement, guaranteed them in nature and recognized in their national constitution. To deprive anyone of his freedom without doing it to restrain from jeopardising the freedom of others is arbitrary to natural dignity and amounts to violent persecution. Otherwise everybody has the right to speak out on any issue as this does not slander the character of others. Freedom of religion is one of the rights guaranteed in liberal and democratic constitutions but which sometimes comes into conflict with them. In Kenya, freedom of worship is always a political issue because of the envy of politicians who like sharing the pulpit with priests to preach development. While church ministers refuse politicians to use the pulpit for personal purposes then there arises the issue of how much the church should participate in politics, economics and modernization without taking power from politicians. Preachers in Kenya have the same professional freedom as civil servants, doctors, teachers and architects and politicians should not expect them to support any partisan ideologies. The preacher's power is to infuence, not to control or endorse. The power of the church consists of telling the truth and practising it in love, morality and justice and not in seeking support from politicians. This is how preaching becomes a national resource.

Hence national leaders whom the clergy are a part should try their best to respect each other's role and profession and cease interfering with each other's ministry and service to the people. In the final analysis all institutions of the national order, including their leaders are there to help people secure better means of existence by making them feel secure in the homes and as citizens.

8.5 ORDER AND CHARISMA

In Kenya, there are movements based on sentimental values which nobody can claim to head and belonging to no specific institution. During the Kenyatta era it appeared as if Kenyatta was the head of the Harambee movement which helped to provide national development with the moral and emotional backing necessary to motivate people offer their money, goods and services. This Harambee movement became so much a part of national order that it needed someone to give it some doctrinal framework. The ideals of Nyayoism, peace, love and unity came in continuity with the national development laid down by President Kenyatta on the basis of Harambee "pulling together" concept.

President Moi, Kenyatta's successor, coined Nyayo to win popular confidence with the people through the transition period and to lay down his own political foundation upon that which was already existing since the country gained independence. President Moi, therefore, recognized the power of his presidency as being more effective in charismatic influence than other ways. With his inclinations to religion and commitment to church life, President Moi had enough charisma from which to draw enough ideals for promoting and motivating loyalty to him in process of development. Moi begun his presidency as a morally committed person with sufficient bodily personality of a fatherly figure, and with visionary goals. His very natural stature epitomized love for children and won him praise by many women organizations. Few could successfully pretend to be Nyayoists without being forced by their conscience to abandon corruption. As the father of the nation, Moi means the father of three children, peace, love and unity.

But do all those who appear to identify themselves with Nyayo philosophy of peace, love and unity share with the president the same values of moral commitment and fear of God as he does? Do all Nyayo followers understand the values of Nyayo philosophy mediated by our president? It appears that many rich and powerful pharisees can pretend to be Nyayo followers and avoid detection for some years, though not for ever.

People with riches seeking blessings from whoever is the president of the republic can undermine Nyayo philosophy. Whether their money is given to assist moral courses or not this is not the problem. The issue is how they gather their money and whether they have paid all their taxes. Some may donate to buy press coverage and win popularity for the next elections, but that is something unavoidable in a democratic system.

Still going further away from Nyayo philosophy is a man who underpays one maid who takes care of his small children, overworks her for eighteen hours a day, and denies her the time to look after her own children. For President Moi, all children are the same and equal, whether they belong to a maid or cabinet minister. How can a Nyayo lover love only his own children and hate those of the men and women who till his land and milk his cows? Nyayoism is not a deliberate ideology to create bad conditions of existence for the majority so that we can raise money to help them. Nyayoism and Harambee spirit should be separated as two separate ideologies when it comes to the rich offering money to buy medicine and build clinics for those with whom they are not united, are at economic wars and do not love. If I wound your leg because I have money to pay for bandages to dress it, won't you prefer that I stop injuring you and keep my bandage?

The idea of love, peace and unity should not therefore be confused with a rich man giving aid to the poor man from whom he stole the money. This is what developed countries do to the poor developing countries from whom they exploit raw materials, cheap labour and cultural values when they give them foreign aid. If we were to practise justice, thus, peace, love and unity the image of an exploiter helping the exploited can disappear. All aid to the poor should be directed at improving our natural order to abolish poverty and misery.

As a small boy, my mother used to take me with her to Sunday School and Church. One Sunday she announced that the next Sunday worship shall be held outside under a tree because the walls of the church building were leaning away from each other and the roof was caving in. She then said the people shall come with some of their harvest for thanksgiving to God because the worship service will be a "Karambii" one. Karambii, from which the Harambee comes, meant that every member of the worshipping community had to bring something toward the construction of a new church. The church building was at that time used as a school classroom from Monday to Friday and therefore even non-Christians came to bring things for Karambii. There was neither a guest of honour nor an announcement of what the individuals brought. Some people promised to flatten the ground, others to dig holes for the poles and others to have poles cut from their gardens. Some offered nails, others thatch grass and others food for workers. I remember myself and many other small boys pledged to jump into the mud hole to knead the mud paste for the walls. There was no individual, acting as an individual who exploited that situation for personal interests. The Karambii was a show of unity, peace and love and not an occasion to get publicity, win votes and get famous. All businessmen, teachers, "tribal" policemen, elders and leaders of the community participated in the same work as the other members of the community.

Our final question is whether all work done in the society by people of different professions is not a Harambee done in a specialized manner. It is the task of those who hold national positions to have their attitudes transformed into a harambee posture so that they conduct their work as a part of the total work of national development.

Some may answer that harambee has lost its charisma due to the quicker development of the vice and slower development of the moral. In every society where the development of physical facilities is more emphasized than moral development you can expect repression, exploitation, dictatorship and falsehood to superceed the development of virtue, peace, love and unity. When the idea of having African bishops, cabinet ministers, doctors, judges and professors became the yardstick of development, aimed more at Africanization than a virtue, vice took advantage of dignity.

Those in the whelms of power must not wait for moral outrage to go to the extent where people have to stone a pick-pocket to death, riot for food, or resign to suffering in order to know that the people have lost faith in themselves and their leaders. For instance, the people had almost given up their trust in justice when a Mombasa judge acquitted a white American sailor convicted of murdering a young black Kenyan woman because justice was not seen to be done. Court charisma cannot be maintained without being supported with right sentences against specific cases.

In order to get satisfied with the dignity of those who hold superior and distinct positions in society, judges, presidents, bishops and others, their performances must pass public approval and accountability, otherwise their power will grow soft from underneath. The days of illiterate popular and emotional movements as instruments of political power are gone. You cannot expect the same call of "Harambee" and response of "Hooooo" to continue today the way it used to be in the 1960's Nowadays people are sober and have forgotten the hang-over of anti-colonial slogans. The people understand that their destinies are no longer in the hands of any single group of politicians but in the hands of elaborate national institutions properly established to survive beyond the survival of any particular regime. Charisma has given way to wisdom and wisdom to stable institutions. Love has produced respect and respect trust. This is a product of independence which in Kenya has grown from infancy to adolescence and from adolescence to full maturity. The distance from colonialism is so great that a majority of Kenyans living now twenty four years after independence did not exist during the first day of independence.

The present generation, and let us not make any bones about it, is freer and existing better than the generations which existed during colonial times. The present population has better access to food, water, transportation, education, medidine, press, legal aid, financial institutions, maternity wards, and other means of existence. There is less violence by police and rulers against those suspected to break the law and may be less torture of arrested suspects than during colonial times.

But any topic on national order is not complete without mentioning the existence of ruling parties of which only one remains in Kenya. The present Kenya African National Union, KANU has been made the only *de jure* party in the republic. The party becomes alive in the press mainly during national elections when clearing candidates and electing its own leaders and at other times when disciplining its disobedient, skeptical and cynical members. Other than the party, churches, school committees, co-operative societies, industries and firms meet with the masses. The party itself concentrates more on the task of ruling and exercise leadership than exciting the masses. The trade union movement which used to excite the masses during the early days of independence has also ceased to go to the streets and works behind doors by means of negotiation. It appears that the Kenya leadership is increasingly abandoning the tactics of charismatic leadership as in the days of Kamukunji's and mass rallies in the 1960's and adopting the strategies of engaging the people in actual constructive programmes of development.

We Kenyans are becoming more and more organized into orderly approach to social problems and less and less open to mass emotions. People admire more the institutionalized politics in which services are community based than handout promises. Besides the party, there are many other organizations making strong appeal to the masses with enlightened approach and reasoning like parents associations and school boards of governors. The institutions that mediate development, especially the churches and co-operative societies do wield a lot of power and solidarity among their members. Whether these institutions are conscious of themselves as being instruments of mediating power and development between the state and the people is not our main problem. The problem which bothers me is what would happen in Kenya if the people were to abandon organized institutions as expressions of their aspirations to dignity and were to return to mob and mass politics of disorganised crowds, masses, personality cults and emotional responses of the 1960's. By the time we have returned to the masses as the centre of national power and focus for democracy the stability of the country will have become completely eroded. We can no longer entrust mass rallies of Kamukunji type to approve programmes of national importance without the technical advice that the parliament requires from various ministries before approving allocation of resources and planning of development. Nevertheless, the masses are still necessary to disapprove unnecessary programmes and unjust behaviour in the system.

Finally, and before coming to any conclusion, let me cite a case outside our own in which politico-economic progress does not necessary mean better existence. In August 1980, the World Youth movement invited me to address a consultation of young people from Europe, Middle East and Africa and with representatives from North America. The consultation took place in Cyprus. During the discussions, I discovered that Africa has less problems of disorder, indignity and vice than the European countries where disorder is so much apart of order that you cannot notice it at one glance.

As the discussions went on and issues of violence, freedom, liberations and dehuminization became hotter, people begun to speak from personal experience. Africans spoke of decolonization, renewal and independence, focussing their attention on the struggle against apartheid in Southern Africa. But no sooner than issues began to sink in our minds Africans began to celebrate their new understanding and to plan new strategies for continued struggle. But the Europeans begun to drink alcohol, take drugs and play sex. While the discussion brought new discoveries and hope to African participants it brought remorse and fatalism to our brothers and sisters from America and Europe. The difference was that while it was foreigners practising violence against Africans in Africa, it was the Americans and Europeans practising violence against themselves in their countries. While we from Africa had left oppression, exploitation and colonialism at home and were enjoying our stay in Cyprus, the Europeans had internalized and assimilated so much homicide, suicide, alcoholism, drug abuse, abortions and other depressive habits against themselves that they could not free themselves.

While Africans were suffering from the known disease of western imperialism and neo-colonialism, the Europeans wre suffering from an unknown domestic disease with serious symptoms of self-destruction. The dignity of a black person fighting for freedom from white domination appèared to be God's blessing in disguise compared with the dehumanization of a middle class youth from Europe and America seeking escape from his unknown disease by injecting himself with drugs to relieve himself of guilt, lack of self-respect, low self-esteem, depression and disillusionment.

The dignity that makes a colonized woman want to bear a son or a daughter with whom to share her plight, a Messiah who will free her from colonialism, shows the highest form of dignity, that is, hope in oneself, in contrast to a so-called civilized American or European woman who feels compulsive desire for sex so that she can abort and kill the future, possibilities of a Messiah. The amount of violence these so-called civilized people in the North can direct against themselves, their unborn children (foetus), including violence consumed through narcotic drugs exceeds the violence they have used against us from the days of slave trade to now. Through abortions alone these countries kill more people per year than they were able to kill in a single year in Vietnam. Their technological and pharmaceutical warfare against themselves is more dangerous than hunger in Africa because hunger can be cured by a known amount of food and end instantly while theirs is a disease of internal collapse of human dignity. It is a disease rarely known in Kenya where in contrast to England we have known agnostics, atheists and homosexuals. These people need our assistance to help them reconstruct their hearts, in order for God, the creator and source of dignity to return. We had a delegate from Uganda who prefered the political turmoil which existed in his country to the spiritual turmoil which exists in Europe. The problem is that while in Uganda has no means to spread its problems to other countries Europe has the international business, missions, press and diplomacy to spread and impose its domestic evils all over the world and with the help of America.

Our just criticism of all forms of power is based on human conscience which is a reflection of our inner dignity. The freedom to criticize and correct social, political and religious excesses of power, and malpractices, abuses, and malfunctions comes from our hearts and not from the police and military. The most just criticism of a system of power is that which comes from the heart of a beggar, sickman, child, downtrodden and oppressed because they do so without the physical and material power to enforce their will. Their criticism is like a prayer offered to God that "They will be done on earth". And God hears their prayers and brings down the mighty crawling on their knees.

It is very dangerous for an ordinary citizen to point at the evils of an officer who draws a huge salary from public service but spends much of his time doing his private work, deploys government tractors to dig his own shamba, uses government medicine in his clinic and uses a government vehicle to transport his domestic workers, and then overcharges his patients and workers for the stolen services. To criticize such an officer is like recruting your own murderer. The lack of dignity in the heart of such an officer leaves a big vacuum that he tries to feel with all kinds of wickedness which may include attempts to assasinate his critics and opponents. Yet we need public criticism in order to arouse the dormant conscience of those who are personally moral but are working in an immoral situation. We have dignified individuals who are too weak to overcome the pressure of others in the system who need our sermons in order to stand firm and to realize that they are not alone. Human dignity responds very positively to criticism and feels strong among the rank and file of corrupt and sinful organization. When a system of evil organizations is criticized in public there are people in it who feel encouraged to repent and reform the system from within. This means that some constructive criticism and opposition from without any specific order, for instance the church, the government, the party or the industry can help those working within to rise up and be counted as against the evils of their system.

Dignity must remain an essential component of national order within the totality of every system by which a country sustains itself. Even in Sodom and Gomorrah God offered the last chance of freedom and escape to people like Lot and his family to show how possible it is to have elements of righteousness in a hopeless situation.

I believe that all people are created in the likeness of God which offered chance, hope and promise and survived even under the most extreme form of exploitation, anarchy and death. Dignity can survive in extreme disorder and become the basis of a new order. It is not for dignity to hold on to a dirty and destructive order for too long. It must allow the disintegration of orders that have gone beyond the capacity to reform themselves as Jesus Christ said about the temple and walls of Jerusalem. Dignity believes in resurrection. Anyone who lives in dignity with other people will live in glory with God.

CHAPTER 9
THE PSALMS OF DIGNITY

"When I look at thy heavens, the work of thy fingers, the moon and the stars which thou has established, what is man that thou art mindful of him, and the Son of man that thou dost care for him. Yet thou has made him little less than God and dost crown him with glory and honour". (Psalm 8: 3-5).

Dignity is the pleasure, delight, satisfaction, love and confidence that we are the Creator's representatives to other creatures and stewards of His creation. We enjoy to be who we are and are happy to be ourselves in this world of struggle against hunger, disease, poverty and evil. Woe unto the modern literature, mass media and music which start where dignity stops and creative work ceases, repeating to us the story of man as a money-maker, sexual maniac, power tyrant, jealous, rebel, criminal lunatic and depressed patient. When I insist that man has dignity, affection, and grace they laugh at me to take my utopia, illusion, fantasy and dream world out of their world. There is not a world where orderly being maters, it is one dominated by having. Therefore, the following partially-formed song of dignity expresses in Psalms what man is and should be as opposed to what he has and should produce. There is so much unspoken dignity remaining in man that I would like the world to notice by reading the following psalms of dignity.

Psalms 1
Dignity, you are the spirit that elevated man above the things he owns and preserves him from the tendency to be like men. In spite of his loses or gains, sickness or health and suffering or pleasure, you are able to sustain man in his own value as a partner of God in the universe. Through dignity you are little less than the glory of God only you reflect the glory, majesty, power and holiness of God in man. You allow man to protect his own image into space and time without becoming enslaved to them. You entrust to man the prudent management of resources and diligent exercise of duty

without letting his soul become one of the resources and duties he has to perform. This independence, self-awareness and freedom to determine other things without being determined by them is what we lose when we bow down to worship the idols that make us to believe that our dignity exists in the gun, palace, automobile, movie, disco, party, title or uniform. Our dignity comes from those we love and help, not from the things we own or produce.

Dignity, you make us agree that we brought nothing to this world and shall take away nothing from it. So, we cannot enjoy dignity by trying to keep it for ourselves. We shall never win dignity by trying to win it like our monthly income. To know and have dignity is to communicate life to others, to respect, esteem and love them. Dignity, we experience you not as things but as people well-grounded in the fear of God and respect for one another.

Dignity, society and its institutions should be nothing but human dignity by extension. We communicate ourselves and reproduce our image through our churches and governments, the schools, the theatre and the hospital are nothing but the mass media of communicating dignity with one another. Dignity, cities, towns and villages reflect in the world the true picture of ourselves. Before anything happens in the streets of Nairobi, Kenyans have already committed it in their own souls. We can ascertain whether the projection of God's image in us is still in us by projecting our own in society. God creates man and in turn man creates society. Society is where we love our neighbours as ourselves and do unto others as we would like them to do unto us.

How grieved, depressed, frustrated, cruel, plastic, devious, crafty, manipulatijve, tyrannical and evil are those who instead of projecting their dignity to others project their fists, swords, atomic bombs, dollars, pounds, titles, position, professional status, age, and other products of worldly success. By contradicting their own dignity they disregard their own nature as God's children and makers of society. What dignity gives, dignity takes away, dust to dust and ashes to ashes like Sodom and Gomorrah. Take away dignity from man, and with it the society goes.

Psalms 2

Dignity, let me delight in my own natural beauty, and rejoice in the clarity, radiance, courage, integrity, honesty, love, humility, patience, endurance, openness, wisdom and justice by which you connect me with my people. Dignity, you have given me the faith and justice to my people. Dignity, you have given me the faith and justice to let others be themselves so that I can be happy to be me and not someone better. Dignity, it is good that you are not a person yourself because I would marry you one after another, for ever and ever.

Psalm 3

Dignity, you are the truth and evidence of my existence. Without you my blood and flesh are not worth more than those of other animals. Anybody can seize my body and torture, imprison, hunger, enslave or possess it but cannot harm by dignity. I rejoice that dignity is a consciousness of mind and soul, in the body. Dignity resists to be a product and rejects being measured by weight, size and volume. Jesus the son of Mary had as much dignity as a child in a manger as he had as an adult on the cross. Dignity is not the product of years of living, working or experience, even though it is formed in us through the struggle for existence. Dignity, I thank you that I am not a copy-cat of my parents nor an imitation of my environment. Thank you that nobody can produce of you exactly what he wants. In each and every person you present a unique reflection of dignity. My dear dignity, I have nothing else for you but songs.

Psalm 4

Dignity, you are the source, the process and the end of meaningful· existence. You love to be enjoyed and not possessed. You want me to enjoy others and not their music, to appreciate donors and not their donations. You know that evil loves the gift and not the giver, likes creation and not the creator and enjoys the fruits of labour and hates the labourer. Dignity, evil is your opposite, your negative, the antithesis of your nature and character. Evil keeps products and discards the producer, accumulates works and reduces workers, inflated prices and deflated consumers, upgrades machines and degrades technicians, and by these works of wickedness deceives people that dignity exists in having things and not in being human.

Dignity, you always remain in people. You are never in the food but in the cooks, not in music but in the composers, not in the vehicles but in the driver, not in the possessions but in the owners. Somebdy can have the world and be evil, without dignity. Your love, or dignity, is complete without sex, your service enough without masters, and your personality perfect without ornaments.

Dignity, you travel long distances to visit the sick, captives, aged and others from whom .you expect no material gain, having affection for those you cannot expect to vote or speak good of you, and kissing those who persecute you. So, dignity, you truly love being and not having, people and not products, life and not achievement. Dignity, you are not how much money can make by exploiting others, but how many people one can use money to help.

Dignity, why are you found in the carpenter and not in his elegant furniture, in the farmer and not in his crops, and in the bankers and not in his money? Dignity, we are amused that you cannot be found in the best and most valuable pieces of property. you can make our positions as parents, lawyers, politicians, soldiers, nurses, drivers, cooks, farmers, businessmen and preachers instruments and means of projectig human dignity in society and not ends in themselves. Does this mean that the president of a country projects more dignity in society than an office messenger, or air captain more dignity than a fisherman? No! What happens is that besides the president and the captain expressing their own personal dignity, they also represent and project the dignity of all the people their positions represent. Their collective and corporate responsibility demands leaders to reflect not only their own dignity but also be identified. Their crimes becomes our crimes and their dignity our dignity. The dignity of those in authority is our dignity and their evil our evil. If leaders go to war, the nation goes to war and if they live in order, the whole country becomes orderly.

Psalm 5

Dignity, helps us to search you in the one who paints and not in his pictures, in the servant and not in the service and in the giver rather than in the gift. We can find you in the one praying and not in prayers. You are not like the treasure that can be burned or destroyed by moth.

Psalm 6

Dignity, you refused to be an ideology for export when Catholics believed you existed in their churches, protestants in their missions, communists in their party and capitalists in their books. You are dynamic, original and creative rather than final and fixed. Unlike finished products, creeds, dogmas and traditions that can be packed for export, dignity is contageous and spreads directly where people respect and serve one another.

Dignity is seen in parents sheltering their children from rain and bad weather, leaders protecting the poor from exploitation, and in the poor not selling the poor. Dignity, you come from my parents kissing me and not from the kiss, from my wife nursing my ego and not from nursing, from my husband listening to me not from the listening. Dignity is therefore not getting anything your way but understanding others in order for them to understand you. Dignity is a father travelling a thousand miles away from business to take home to a child a toy which would have cost him a few coins to post. Dignity, you are a game, a drama and a play which nobody enjoys in ideologies without getting involved. You are a game which only participants can enjoy and outside the experience of spectators. Dignity, you are personal and not mass.

Psalm 7

Dignity, your glorious, meek, silent, gracious and peaceful presence in our country flows like rivers of righteous-ness, patience, justice, forgiveness, tolerance and love. You have given hope to the lame, young, sick, oppressed, hungry, alienated, marginalized, poor and exiled whom our wicked minds call drop-outs. All those are your people. You use them to form national dignity.

203

Psalm 8

Dignity, you have experienced sorrow, grief and pain. That is why you are strongly aroused and made indignant by those who kill orphans, widows and widowers, aged and others without close relatives. Dignity, you can part with the grief of the departed and let buried the corpse because you have never confined their dignity to their bodies.

Psalam 9 Dignity, I have travelled with you long distances of freedom, happiness, justice and hope beyond the limits sinners put on your way by their racism, bombs, warships, hatred and taboos. Those who erect the barriers of colour, sex, iron curtains, prejudice, discrimination and class on your path to justice and peace discover that you are not one of their old time religious and archaic Christianity. This makes you universal and ecumenical.

Psalm 10

Dignity, is more "agape" than eros. It loves to share what it has with everybody even those who have nothing with which to reciprocate. It shares everything it has in order to avoid the jealousy and enemity of the have-nots. The bearer of dignity receives his character from whether he is on the throne or in bed. Dignity never becomes too rich to the point where the principles of love and justice give way to self-glorification with profits that endanger the profits of another. Without this kind of dignity in which self-interests are subservient to common interests the society builds a nation of mansions, roads, castles, skyscrapers, clubs, banks and armies at the expense of exploiting the people.

Psalm 11

Dignity harmonizes polarization and confrontation by resolving contradictions, reconciling the opposites, reducing the tension and paying the debt and putting the contraries in one stream. Dignity binds together old enemies, opponents and rivals by seeking alternatives than by being neutral and pious. It finds the necessary material for unity in the existing divisions, conflicts and violence. It sides with nobody but appears to side with the poor, weak, oppressed, downtrodden, conquered and defeated. The aim of siding with victims of colonialism, exploitation or oppression is not to become a victim but to join the weaker side of the evil system, thus, to break evil at its weakest link. It is easier to destroy the master-slave relationship by joining forces with the slaves but very difficult to stop the slave becoming the new master once the old master is gone. Unlike dignity which aims at complete destruction of colonized-colonizer relationship, the colonized, in his own self-interest, is full of the evils of the colonizer and desires to replace the colonizer by being the new colonizer. After a hundred years since the abolition of *de jure* slavery, you can observe the existence of *facto* slavery perpetuated by former slaves and their offspring. There is a tendency of losers to think that dignity exists in winners, that the end justifies the means.

Psalm 12
Dignity is the reward and fruit of seeking the good of others. Dignity is the wages of affirming the identity of others and helping them to destroy their negative identities. It helps liberate and free from domination, tradition, custom, law and taboo the person these hold down as the property of another. In this process dignity prefers the properties of a prophet, messiah and liberator and endures a lot of violence, disorder, chaos, anarchy, death, conflicts, tensions and confrontation. Dignity does not hide its own pain when the foxes are feasting and the chicken bleeding, when some people behave like foxes and treat others like chicken. Dignity is peace in the people themselves and not peace in a place where people are handicapped to stop reacting. Pain relieving pills cannot substitute for justice. It is antithetical to all principles of human dignity to pacify a human being into accepting his loss of freedom, expression and dignity as the condition for peace, law and order. Order is an affirmation of dignity.

Psalm 13
Dignity keeps marriage surviving even after the priests and judges have granted the couple a legal divorce. This is because dignity repents and forgives others at its own accord. Dignity

provides children to the homes of barren parents, and makes the weak last longer than the strong. Dignity accepts to pay the losses in a conflict.

Psalm 14
Dignity is not a truth, a doctrine or a religion that need not suffer hunger, oppression or heat. It is a soul that experiences what the body experiences. Dignity endures crisis the body cannot, manifests itself in the visible bodies of those who suffer in fellowship with one another. Dignity your sorrow about the pathetic filth of the rich who still milk from bottles addressed to the poor children is written on the faces of righteous people. Your tears drop from the eyes of just men like rain mourning the dead whose blood was by injustice like water by a sponge. Dignity, your heart is broken by the ideologies of city planners, priests, scientists, artists, philosophers and politicians who organise everything to suit themselves at the expense of the people.

Psalm 15
Dignity, you hate the self-love of the super-powers that looks the naked bodies of malnutrited children in order to donate token proofs of their "false dignity". They work the bodies of miners into skeletons so that they can grant them. You cannot be found in those who hurt so that they can provide them bandages or those who kill parents so that they can have orphans to put in their orphanages. This perversion of moral and religious values by the super-rich who replace human dignity with charity is what perpetuates foreign missions and peace-corps. Their interest is to squeeze out every drop of dignity from the people so that they can dish it out as famine relief and aid for development.

Dignity, you dislike the animal-care some nations give others and the machine-care some dehumanized people receive from their dehumanizers. Do not rob somebody his dignity and then pretend to restore it with charity. Charity should be an instrument of dignity but not a substitute.

Psalm 16
Dignity, you are the power that makes us aware that we have

souls and the influence that causes others to love us. Those who have no dignity cannot see dignity in others. Instead of respecting others the evil men fear them. Those who fear others see them as something greater than God. But Jesus discouraged this substitution of love with fear and said "Fear not them that can kill the body but cannot kill the soul. Fear God who can kill both the body and the soul."

Psalm 17
Dignity is a friend to all. It welcomes everyone into its room, offices, homes, recreation and place without conditions. All guests of the Almighty God are guest of dignity in this world. Dignity offers like-loooking of coffee and tea to all who need their sense of worth re-awakened, and their sense of belonging affirmed. Dignity, you are very angry with the fear of popes, patriarchs, moderators, chiefs, priests and politicians and professionals who cannot eat with anybody alien to their religion, tribe, class or family. Dignity, you use uniform procedures, laws, practices and customs for your social order.

Psalm 18
Dignity discovered sin in the multiple stratification of schools system in different classes of cost while offering the same examinations. Dignity cannot enjoy putting the lions of higher cost schools together with the sheep of lower cost ones in the same job market to compete for survival. You cannot compete with the same speed with people runing on tarmac while you run on gravel

Psalm 19
Dignity, you are not afraid of speaking out against the consciences of generals, bishops, magnates, tycoons, despots and tyrants who think that you could be completely rooted out of their souls. O dignity, you are still found in the hearts where evil exists, condemning as foul sinners and nothings those who appoint themselves as righteous, democratic, saints, pious, just and peaceful with their mouths while their actions speak to the contrary. You hate these peope who act like ambulances to pick up the victims of their exploitation.

207

Psalm 20
Dignity, you abhor those powerful Hitlers, Amins, Bokassas, dictators and criminals who spend sleepless nights planning how to come back to power after their power has collapsed like an overspeeding horse without control or direction.

Psalm 21
My dignity, you have suffered for too long the agony of being lectured and preached at that "all men are created equal" by the same lecturers and preachers who imprisoned and detained you to prevent you realizing and implementing their sermons and lectures. They talk of equal laws, opportunities, lectures, sermons, and verbalism but not in history and reality where everybody demands them to share comforts.

Psalm 22
The dignified ones are the disciples of Christ. They are never too good for this world. Their goal is heaven and their task is the world. The disciples, not the Christians, those who are like Christ in their dignity, not in their religion, are the most indispensable necessity of world dignity. Their dignity is the highest good and the supreme value which the earth possess, for without them the value of human life will be turned into the material value of coffee, gold, diamond and oil. It is these outcasts, the disciples of dignity who are the salt and light of the world that penetrates without compromise. Every society needs the disciples of dignity who do not only enjoy dignity but can sacrifice themselves for it like in the food. We cannot have good world trade, religion and system without world dignity based on national dignities.

Psalm 23
Diginity speaks to the world from small people as well as great ones. *All people are great in one way and small in another.* God has strange ways of letting his dignity to shine in both small and big places. He let it shine in Bethlehem in a manger Dignity has curious ways of expressing its power and influence through ordinary people like fishermen, shepherds and children. The rays of dignity radiate from the toiling lives of nobodies to whom our secular and religious scheme of

values accords no dignity. The debased and dehumanized wretched of the earth who do not seem to matter to the multinational companies and the corporate directors live and die in the dignity of God. Those who looked for dignity in fat money, big armies, mafia gangs, big houses and huge possessions died on the roads without God and far from their dignity. Dignity, you are a serene, calm and sweet settlement in the hearts of cooks in the kitchen, the cribs of babies and shanty dwellers. You may never be found in the cerebrities, rich and powerful who think of dignity as headlines. Dignity is not a bank account or many wives.

Psalm 24
Dignity, you may be found in those we call master, leader, teacher, pastor and parent, not because they told us to call them so but because they make us feel dignified, safe and secure.

Psalm 25
Dignity, how glorious are the faces of those in whose hearts you dwell. They talk to us with authority without any intimidation and make us follow them without coercion. We can instinctively pray for them and recognize the power of god in them. We can trust their command and know that it is safe to obey them. They guide us and rule our country because we have given them our consent. These are the leaders who like good shepherds volunteered to die for us, suffer and be detained, without first seeking guarantee that we shall make them saints, heroes and leaders. They are the models of our national identity. They are clothed with our good customs, laws and traditions.

Psalm 26
Dignity, you are fond of forgiving law-breakers, thieves, rebels, "revolutionaries" and the "woman caught in adultery'" because you have found those entrusted with law, justice and order themselves being lawless, unjust and disorderly and as much is need of dignity as their opponents. Better those who admit that they need dignity than those who are too self-

righteous to admit they lack any. I wonder why self-righteousness prefers to be overthrown by force than admit guilt and be hanged than yield to criticism. Self-righteousness is total self-interest which suspends reason and justice when these serve the general and common interests.

Psalm 27
Dignity wonders with what justice can a man claim the labour of another and create social conditions which justifies misery for the unborn who will belong to his labourers. What humanity allows one to destroy the dwellings of a slum dweller in the name of hygiene as if the slum dwellers preferred shanties to castles, maisonettes, bangalows and mansions. Did some people choose something worse when something better was available? Why does indignity display wealth and inflex its muscles before the eyes of the wretched people who demand water to drink and bread to eat.

Psalm 28
Dignity exercise its freedom to choose between alternative available and may choose death rather than self-compromise. Dignity refuses being a victim of the choices made yesterday if they negate the freedom to make new ones. Today dignity may choose to compromise some of its characteristics, like order for justice, peace for love and respect for integrity but will not forget to have them back after victory. Dignity discards the laws of convenience and opportunism that take advantage of other people's weaknesses. Not that dignity likes weakness, poverty and sickness, but that it moves like wind, from high to low pressure.

Psalm 29
Dignity lifts above Sabbath, church and state the sacredness of human life. Dignity moves low in order to lift high those who have lost honour, respect and freedom, "as Christ loved the church and gave Himself for her." Ephesians 5:25. What you offer to your family, education, housing, clothes, food, service, support, protection, entertainment and property is not enough until you have offered yourself. God used to visit and be with Adam and Eve despite the word He

had given them and sent his only Son Jesus Christ to be with his people and die for them in spite of having given them other things. Dignity is touching somebody with your life, giving life for life. Dignity takes nothing as of any value until the person offering it to his family or country offers himself together with it.

Dignity wonders how long women will hang on to men for mercy, protection and support due to men's self-interests. Procreation cannot give justification to oppress women because even female animals and trees which do the work of procreating their kind do not become inferior to male animals and trees. Human dignity is women participating in procreation in order to perpetuate their own dignity by projecting themselves in the future generations. Dignity is women worth men and men worth women and not each giving something to the other. "The two shall become one" does not mean one buying the other or one receiving goods and services from his or her partner. Partnership means being joined to each other as men and women where none joins the property of the other. There is nothing in heaven or on earth with which one can buy another without lowering his or her dignity and reducing it to a commodity. God Himself never offered angels or gold to redeem man but offered Himself to prove that only God owns the secret to the dignity of man.

Psalm 30
Dignity gains from the lessons of the past, learns from ancestral traditions, treads on known ways and seeks freedom from them in order to create possibilities for a better and new day. Dignity is apart of our past experiences in slavery and colonialism and uses our negative experience of defeat, loss, pain or failure as booster rockets to propel us to a new future. While we owe our lives to the future, to the past we owe nothing except thanks.

Psalm 31
Dignity calls it high time for African men and women to unite with each other to bring to an end the diseases of shame guilt and dependence that swindle married people their dignity. The day has come when the worth of a woman is in her total

211

personality, body, mind and soul and not in her make-ups, dresses and style. Women must be distinguished by their own thoughts, self-confidence, pride and faith and not by their dowries, recipes, fashions and baby nappies. The majority of sycho-somatic sickness in Kenya shall disappear when women shall find fulfillment in being complete human beings without the need for additional materials from witchdoctors, astrologers, magicians and conmen who call themselves gentlemen in order to elevate themselves above women. There is no dignity in a gentleman whose woman is so dependent on him that she keeps on threatening to leave him in case he loses his income or dies and leaves her without support. Dignity is being needed because of who you are but not because you hold others hostage by your possessions. There is as much dignity in womanhood in being singles as in being married in being a widow as in marriage.

Psalm 32
Dignity is its own genesis. It sees nothing beautiful in borrowed images and imitations. To an African who accepts his own physical appearance as the one fit for his dignity, dignity rewards him with pride, satisfaction and self-respect and to the one who transforms his face to hide blackness dignity curses him with self-hate and inferiority complex. Dignity is proud of historical record and tells its children that having been in slavery under the Egyptians, Babylonians, British, French or American whites was a problem of some having more military hardware and being more advanced in the art of war, but had nothing to do with having greater dignity more advanced in human value.

Psalm 33
May the God of dignity who made man His own dignity never get tired of restoring dignity to all those who repent of their petty- self-interests that confuse people with things, and dignity with commodity. God's dignity represents his love for mankind. This love of God reflects itself in us when we love even those who fail to show us love in return. When we love those who love us, our brethren, our nation, our friends, our kith and kins, we are no different from wild dogs and hyenas

which do the same to animals of their own den and kind. Christ showed us what dignity means by giving his life for us, the righteous dying for the unrighteous, the just for the unjust, the strong for the weak and the rich for the poor.

Psalm 34

As brother stands by brother in distress, sister by sister binding up her wounds, so let us show our love towards our enemies by "praying for them that persecute us". For it is more blessed to give than to receive. Dignity cannot be confined to our politics, nationalism, religion, economics race and sex but sets out to build the kingdom of heaven on earth, and in so doing ignores ideological boundaries. Dignity is a hidden righteousness. Dignity is a prayer that invites God's kingdom to come and replace our own power and others. Dignity is listed and certified by recognizing others dignity and by never seeking recognition for itself. Do not look for dignity in the diplomas, possessions and positions you have been able to accumulate for yourself but in what joy or misery you have caused others in the process of achieving them.

Indeed dignity is the highest form of being a human being and is what gives value the bodily existence of human being. There are no human standards to measure its value. Dignity is the spirit of man which shuns death by enduring it and overoming its power by resurrection. Without this faith of resurrection human beings are at the mercy superior animals endowed with superior intellectual faculties and only better than other things in their quantities of intellect. Only the people who accept to suffer martyrdom in their struggle for the dignity of others, who accept loss for the gain of others, and who invest their present for the future of others epitomize dignity.

Psalm 35

O dignity of my dignity, the soul of my soul and love of my love, how beautiful is the nation whose life is dignity. That nation walks not alone but with God. Her people ever to embrace one another in fellowship, come what may.

Psalm 36

In his final hymn of human dignity the Psalmist sings that his human rights consist of both bodily and social rights. Neither social rights nor bodily rights are more important than the others. National life is as valuable as individual life. The kingdom is the people and the people are the kingdom. All are priests, princes, princesses, kings and queens. Everyone is royal.

But what comes first, the chicken or the egg, thus human bodily rights or human social rights? Should a society allow its national identity to go into extinction simply because some of its members want to die of alcoholic, narcotic or sexually transmitted diseases like AIDS? If somebody is suffering an epidemic disease, several mental depression or drug-addiction should the society compel him to seek treatment? Or should the society allow itself to disintegrate because individuals have bodily rights? Or should individuals suffer because their community wants to perpetuate outmoded ways of living like nomadic, feudal, racist, tribal and unhygienic patterns of existence? Should Mrs. Dignity of femininity be allowed by Mr. Dignity of manhood to pursue her feminine claims at the expense of their marriage partnership?

Dignity! Are not your bodily rights in conflict with your dignity when your body depends on chemicals such as alcohol, nicotin, caffein, sleeping pills and narcotics in order to feel normal? Is not your integrity eroded by over-eating, malnutrition, poverty and ignorance? Of course, too much alcohol in your blood impairs your bodily stamina and degrades mental capacities to accept shameful social and psychological behaviour. Bodily rights like drunkeness degenerate the nervous system, cause industrial and road accidents, lead to economic and family breakdown and ruin ones bodily and social dignity.

Should the society allow people to commit suicide, rape, self-mutilation and violence to their own bodies? Or should it allow individuals to spread diseases by their sexual habits and unclean living? Is it a violation of privacy for the village chief to go and kill rats and mosquitoes in somebodies' home? When can individuals sue the state?

Dignity! Dignity is your way of keeping the equilibrium between the bodily rights and social rights so that individuals can live in peace with one another. Your bodily needs, shelter, food, clothing, association, affection, worship, respect and honour can only be met in a society where you recognize that others have the same needs. Neither self-abuse by suicide, alcoholism, narcotics addition, sex mania and overreacting, repression, injustice, restrictions of expression and discrimination contribute to your human dignity.

Dignity! There are problems that confront your body and your society, all at once. In case of military invasion from outside what rights take priority, bodily safety or national security? Should the individual flee away or should he be compelled to take arms and defend the country? If a person should never be forced to kill himself why should be be forced to face death in a war? Of course soldiers face death in dignity because theirs is voluntary service. But should the society coerce somebody willing to serve it as a pastor, teacher, farmer, doctor or athlete to serve it in ways he or she is not willing? A pregnant woman endangers her life for the baby, a prophet his life for the truth and a freedom fighter for freedom. Has the nation the final verdict on causes for which individuals must expose themselves to injuries, possible loss of bodily organs and death? Or do altruistic individuals have rights to enter burning buildings to rescue children? Is there freedom of conscience? What comes first, rights to food, medicine and education or rights to wealth, power and prestige?

Dignity! What shall you do with bodily rights that are in conflict with social rights? Should a passenger smoke his tobacco in front of other train or bus passengers? What about social rights that conflict with other social rights like the conflict between whites and blacks in South Africa. What about human rights when a society sanctions a person kill another as happens during capital punishment? Both capital punishment and wars of aggression are premedicated murder and extreme

215

expressions of social sickness and indignity.

Dignity! You are sure that there is no human dignity without human rights. Human rights are bodily and social private and public, individual and national, like two sides of the same coin. Democracy is an attempt to preserve the integrity of bodily rights in social rights. In democracy all are kings, queens, all are priests and prophets, all are rulers. In this democratic dignity people learn to uphold the dignity of each other by common means of existence, respect and honour of one another. This produces a cultural, religious and political order in which all interact freely. The rights of society, in individuals and nature form a good ecosystem where everybody and everything, including forests and animals, has rights. Nobody goes to ruin a lion or cut a tree for the sake of it, because everything in creation has dignity.

Dignity! Thank you for teaching us that where people have dignity their nation has dignity, their institutions and environment have dignity, their people are happy, and their towns clean. People elect some of themselves to become the state, which is God's ally in protecting human rights. The state becomes peoples instrument of justice in God's hands. This work of God in the hands of the state to lift the human burden of security and protection from everybody, leaves everybody free to enjoy work, rest, sex, smell, food, sleep, clothing, warmth, hearing, learning, movement and recreation without unnecessary worry.

Dignity! Never forget that your bodily happiness, security, freedom and affection go hand in hand with social order. Your safety, peace and service must not jeopardise that of anybody else. For this reason, you cannot allow yourself to drive when drunk, pollute the environment with your vehicle and industry, riot, exhale smoke to others, produce children you cannot feed and educate or fight others. Your presence is a good habitation for all living and non-living things that do not threaten your life.

Dignity! You are extremely conscious of your bodily restrictions in sickness, imprisonment, depression, ignorance and death. You are lucky to be found in the bodily life for more than 70 years. This restriction is natural for those whose bodies are affected by disease and old age and social for those affected by injuries, crimes and murders, that come due to social causes and disorder. These dangers to the body that limit our life-span make us humble enough to handover to the youth our properties, knowledge, offices, positions and goodwill. But the whole process in which dignity exists in the bodily and social life no power on earth, not even a person himself or state should interfere with the natural unity of body and life for any reason whatsoever. Human order is for restricting, by custom, law, tradition and religion human behaviour but not human life. The government, by due process of law in courts may restrict your behaviour and confine it in prison for life, but your bodily rights to be fed, given medical treatment and communicate with other human beings cannot be taken away by yourself or society. The right of the life to be in the body or the body to retain life is the creator's own right. Human rights to possess life and sustain it are above the law. Jesus said "The law was made for man and not man for the law." The social state by which people protect their own life as a society belong to living people and cannot be excused to kill any of them. Soon or later life gains the upper hand of nature and leaves this worldly existence for a higher dignity beyond our social and bodily dignity. God will be the judge of who to enjoy a new dignity of God's glory and who lost this reward by his indignified conduct on earth.